Speaking with Spirit

Published by Ra Sekhi Arts Temple

First Edition Sept 2013

Cover Design by Itiopiya@gmail.com

ISBN-13: 978-1499228342

ISBN-10: 1499228341

19.95

Speaking With Spirit

A compilation of prayers from Afrika and the Diaspora

Published by Ra Sekhi Arts Temple
Edited by Mut Shat Shemsut-Gianprem
May 2014

This book is dedicated to the children of Afrika. May the prayers in the book be medicine to restore and heal your soul.

Table of Contents

Forward	*7*
Praise and Adoration to the NETERU	*10*
Invocations to ORISHA	*39*
Oriki	*47*
Propitations to Ori	*65*
More prayers from Afrika	*72*
Prayers from the Diaspora	*78*
Prayers for Libation	*92*
Prayers for Special Areas	*105*
Meditation	*146*
Final thoughts	*153*

Preface

The power of the word is one of the most powerful and creative forces on the planet. The power of prayer is infinite. We use prayers to connect with our higher self and to that which is Divine.

We have used prayers, chants, song, mediations, and other means of connecting to Spirit since the beginning of time to bring balance, joy, spiritual power and to do so much throughout the ages. In this book, it is our intention to continue this tradition by sharing some of the most powerful and healing prayers we have found in our experiences.

We have included melanated prayers for melanated people. We are unsure of the origins of some of the prayers. We pray that no one is offended by seeing their work included. I was inspired to create this book after speaking with some young people last year who told me they didn't know how to pray, It is our intention to share this work as a means to bring guidance and blessings to those in need, and to continue our tradition of Speaking with Spirit.

May this work be for the highest good of us all.

Forward

Ancient teachings of Jhuty – who some know as Hermes – tell us that THE ALL IS MIND. The One Most High known by many names by many people created the omniverse with a thought and that thought IS the omniverse. Both the Creator and creation is ultimately thought-forms manifest.

This truth of creation reveals the power of prayer. Prayer is the process by which we use our mental powers to co-create the reality of our heart's desire. It is a sacred act of communion with the Omniversal Creator to express our heart's desire.

Communion is like communication – it is multi-faceted and involves articulating, listening, and interpretation. When we articulate what we intend and feel with precision to others there is little room for misinterpretation. When we listen intently to what one is saying, we know how to respond in a way that uplifts and affirms. This applies to communication amongst people as well as communion with the omniverse. So prayer is actually one part of communion. Prayer is articulating heart's desire to the omniverse; meditation is listening to and interpreting omniversal response.

So prayer is half of the equation – meditation – periods of quietness with a stilled mind is the balance. A quiet mind is necessary to receive the inspiration that will empower us to co-create answers to our prayers. Moreover, prayer and meditation should not be compartmentalized. We should do our best to live MIND-FULLY. Mindfullness, always being aware and in control of our thoughts, should be a way of life. Why? – because as Jhuty teaches us – THE ALL IS MIND. Let us do our best to stay prayerful and receptive to communion and inspiration at all times!

Many indigenous cultures feel that the One Most High known by many people and many names is too busy creating universes and galaxies to be focused on the concerns of us microcosmic humans. However, to ensure that we are protected and sustained within omniversal law, the One Most High known by many names and many peoples appointed elements, angels, and ancestors to intercede and answer prayer. This belief has been portrayed by some as polytheism, false idolatry, praying to creation and not the creator, paganism, etc. We should recognize that doctrines that deny our indigenous teachings are often control mechanisms to cut us off from our powers.

We should always be reverent of the One Most High known by many names and many peoples. All praise is due! However, let us not get spooked out of our powers. Honor ancestors, feed ancestors – they are the eyes, ears, and spokespersons for the OMH. Honor the elements of creation – Earth, Air Fire and Water – they are sacred and come together as one in us! Commune with the elements – they are alive and conscious and appointed to answer prayer. There are inter-dimensional Starbeings from the Heavens some call angels who have been appointed to protect us and the planet. Ask and we shall receive. Don't forget the plant and animal kingdoms also have powers to answer prayer as well if we open our minds enough to receive from them.

Because All is Mind, an amazing thing occurs when collectives use the same prayer generation after generation. A powerful field of mental energy is created that augments all who share in the prayer. Each other's prayer augments one another's prayers. This truth reveals the powers of this book *Speaking with Spirit.* Give thanks Nia Yaa and members of the Ra Sekhi Temple for being receptive and obedient to inspiration and bringing answers to prayers.

Ras Ben

Author, Rocks of Ages

A Prayer for Endarkenment

THOU who art Blacker
Than a trillion midnights;
Whose eyes shine brighter
Than a billion suns.

THOU whose hair doth
Coil tighter than a
Million springs, radiating
All energy throughout
The universe.

We beseech THEE, ONE
And ONLY ONE

To give us total strength
to carry out THY will for the universe!

To establish JUSTICE on
planet Earth and live in PEACE.

Dr. Frances Cress Welsing, M.D

Author, The Isis Papers

Praise and Adoration to the NETERU

The Great Forces of Ancient Kemet

THE NETERU

The Neteru are the deities of Ancient Kemet. They are aspects of the Creator. There are hundreds of Neteru. Here are some of the Neteru that have been included in this book, and their attributes.

NTR is a name for THE MOST HIGH, The Source of ALL

AMEN is the all-seeing, all-knowing One

RA/RAAT is the energy of the Sun, the energy that sustains us, an aspect of THE Most High

MAAT is Goddess of the virtues of truth, justice, righteousness, order, reciprocity, harmony and balance.

TEHUTI is the God of wisdom and intelligence

AUSET is the great Mother, nurturer, healer, protector

NEBTHET is the sister of AUSET, healer associated with time, space, imagination, intuition, dreams

AUSAR is The Great Father, husband/brother to Auset, represents highest consciousness

HERU is the son of Auset and Ausar, represents courage, strength, determination, strong will

SEKHMET is the Great Mother Healer and Destroyer of Evil

THE OPENING OF THE WAY

This prayer is done first thing in the morning. It gives praises to the Neteru of the directions and elements and is a way to raise that energy within.

NEBTHET and HAPI in the east represent the lungs and the air element.

SERKET and QEBSUNNEF in the south represent the small intestines and the fire element.

AUSET and AMSET in the west represent the liver and the water element.

NIT and DUAMUTEF in the north represent the large intestines, stomach and the earth element.

NUT represents the sky, GEB the earth

SHU represents air, TEFNUT represents moisture

PAUT NTRU are all NETERU/deities

MBU NTRU is the God force within

Before beginning take a few deep breaths and center yourself.

Begin with chanting ANKH 3 times with arms crossed over your heart.

When saying Anedj-rak (praise and adoration) arms should be in Dua pose, with left hand and left foot forward.

When saying Anuk cross arms over heart.

When saying DUA NTR (Adorations to The Most High)

arms are in Dua pose.

Chant ANKH once at the end of the prayer.

Facing the East begin (lungs/air)	*ANEDJ-RAK NEBT-HET* *ANUK NEBT-HET* *ANEDJ-RAK HAPI* *ANUK HAPI* *DUA-UR NTR*
Turn to the South (small intestine/fire)	*ANEDJ-RAK SERQET* *ANUK SERQET* *ANEDJ-RAK QEBSENNUF* *ANUK QEBSENNUF* *DUA-UR NTR*
Turn to the West (liver/water)	*ANEDJ-RAK AST ANUK AST* *ANEDJ-RAK AMSET ANUK AMSET* *DUA-UR NTR*
Turn to the North (large intestine & stomach/earth)	*ANEDJ-RAK NIT ANUK NIT* *ANEDJ-RAK DUAMUTEF ANUK DUAMUTEF* *DUA-UR NTR*
Facing the East Raise arms over head for NUT, Bend and touch ground for GEB Turn in circle to the right for SHU Turn in circle to the left for TEFNUT	*ANEDJ-RAK ANUT ANUK NUT* *ANEDJ-RAK GEB ANUK GEB* *DUA-UR NTR* *ANEDJ-RAK SHU ANUK SHU* *ANEDJ-RAK TEFNUT* *ANUK TEFNUT* *DUA-UR NTR*
Raise arms up for Paut NTRW (all Neteru) Cross arms over your heart for Nbu NTRW (God force within)	*ANEDJ-RAK PAUT NTRW* *ANUK PAUT NTRW* *ANEDJ-RAK MBU NTRW* *ANUK MBU NTRW* *DUA-UR NTR*

KEMETIC LIBATION

Song: Enen A.....Neter. I ta em Keprah ankh.

Translation

Homage to nature who comes as all aspects of life.

Posture: Kneel Right knee on floor, left knee up with foot on ground. Left hand raised, thumb under ring finger. Right Hand over heart or use ancestral stick to tap the floor

Pouring water on the ground

Anech Hrauk Atef MUT NETER

I ta em Paut Neteru Paut Shepsu

Anech Hrauk MUT UR NUT

Anech Hrauk SHU TUAU

Anech Hrauk SHEKHMET

Anech Hrauk ISEER

Anech Hrauk TEHUTI EN SESHET

Anech Hrauk SEKER-T Tuau

Anech Hrauk MAAT Tuau

Anech Hrauk HERUKUTI- Tuau

Anech Hrauk HERU

Anech Hrauk Mut HET HERU

Anech Hrauk ANPU

Anech Hrauk Mut AUSET

Anech Hrauk GEB- Tuau

Anech Hrauk (Personal Ancestors-- Name who ever you want)

Complete with clap 3 times with right palm over left palm, left palm up.

Translation

I honor the Father Mother Divine

Who come as the Divinity in all forms and the Esteemed Ancestors.

Homage to Great Mother Nut, Tuau calabash of existence.

Homage to the Opener of the way who stands at the crossroads of heaven and earth, and my head and heart, thank you for clarity.

Homage to the Mother of Power, Breath of Life and Transformation.

Homage to the divine within, my source of peace, thank you.

Homage to Tehuti and Seshet for divine wisdom and mystery teachings, thank you.

Homage to the Elder Mother of power for Understanding, thank you.

Homage to the Mother who orders the universe and raises us to spiritual maturity.

Homage to the Magnified Light for teaching us courage to act in truth and extreme light. Protect us, thank you.

Homage to the light of the sun within let our will to make choices be aligned with our true selves thank you.

Homage to the Mother who is the House that bore the light and for Joy within.

Honor to our inner guide and perception, thank you.

Thank you Mama, the light in the dark, for healing and the middle path.

Honor to the spirit of the Earth and the vehicle for this body, thank you.

Submitted by Ayele Kumari

Kemetic Libation

Antcha herak Atef Amen

Antcha herak Mut Amenet

Antcha herak Ra

Antcha herak Rait

Antcha herak Ptah

Antcha herak Sekhmet

Antcha herak Atem

Antcha herak Ausaaset Nebet Hetepet

Antcha herak Ausaaset Nebet Pet

Antcha herak Khepra

Antcha herak Maa

Antcha herak Maat

Antcha herak Tehuti

Antcha herak Seshat

Antcha herak Ausar

Antcha herak Auset

Antcha herak Set

Antcha herak Nebt Het

Antcha herak Heru

Antcha herak Uatchet (Wadjet)

Antcha herak Nekhebet

Antcha herak Heru Behdet

Antcha herak Het Heru

Antcha herak Amen Men

Antcha hera ten Ntorou nebu

Antcha hera ten Ntorotu nebu

Antcha hera ten Aakhu

Antcha hera ten Aakhutu

I na kher ten

Sa setem a, ma setem ten

Sa maa a, ma maa ten

Tuau a

Translation

Homage to you Atef (Father) Amen

Homage to you Mut (Mother) Amenet

Homage to you Ra, Rait, Ptah, Sekhmet, Atem, Ausaaset, Nebet Hetepet, Ausaaset Nebt Pet, etc.

Homage to all (nebu) of the Gods (Ntorou - 'Neteru')

Homage to all (nebu) of the Goddesses (Ntorotu)

Homage to all of the Honored Ancestors (Aakhu) and Ancestresses (Aakhutu)

I have come to you (I na kher ten)

Make me to hear like you hear

Make me to see like you see

I thank you (tuau a)

By Kwesi Ra Nehem Ptah Akhan

Hymn to Ra

Homage to thee, O RA,

when thou rises as TEM-HERU-KHUTI.

Thou art to be adored.

Thy beauties are before mine eyes,

Thy radiance is upon my body.

Thou goest forth to thy setting in the Sektet Boat with fair winds, and thy heart is glad;

The heart of the Matet Boat rejoices.

Thou glides over the heavens in peace,

and all thy foes are cast down;

the stars which never rest sing hymns of praise unto thee,

and the stars which are imperishable glorify thee

as thou sets to rest in the horizon of Manu,

O RA who art beautiful at morn and at eve,

O RA who lives, and are established,

O RA, Homage to thee,

O thou who art KHEPERA when thou rises

and who are Tem when thou sets in beauty.

Thou rises and shines on the back of thy mother NUT,

O RA who art crowned the king of the gods!

Nut welcomes thee, and pays homage unto thee,

and MAAT, the everlasting and never-changing goddess, embraces thee at noon and at eve.

Thou glides over the heavens, being glad at heart, and the Lake of Testes is content.

The gods of the South, the gods of the North, the gods of the West, and the gods of the East praise thee,

O thou Divine Substance, from whom all living things came into being.

O RA, who dwell in heaven before ever the earth and the mountains came into being.

Homage to thee, RA

Only One, thou maker of the things that are,

thou hast fashioned the tongue of the Neteru

Let me breathe the air which cometh forth from thy nostrils, and the north wind which cometh forth from thy mother Nut.

Make my Spirit-soul to be glorious,

O RA thou art exalted by reason of thy wondrous works.

Shine with the rays of light upon my body day by day

Praise be unto thee

O RA exalted Sekhem

Dua

From The Book of Coming Forth by Day (The Book of the Dead)

Hymn to Ausar

Homage to thee, Ausar, Lord of eternity, King of the Gods,

Whose names are manifold,

Whose forms are holy,

Thou being of hidden form in the temples, whose Ka is holy.

Thy name is established in the mouths of men.

Thou art the substance of the Two Lands.

Thou art Tem, the feeder of Kau, the Governor of the Companies of the NTRU.

Thou art the beneficent Spirit among the spirits.

NU of the Celestial Ocean draws from thy waters.

Thou sends forth the north wind at eventide, and breath from thy nostrils to the satisfaction of thy heart.

The stars in the celestial heights are obedient unto thee, and the great doors of the sky open themselves before thee.

Thou art to whom praises are ascribed in the southern heaven, and thanks are given for thee in the northern heaven.

The imperishable stars are under thy supervision, and the stars which never set are thy thrones.

Offerings appear before thee at the decree of GEB.

The Companies of the Gods praise thee, and the gods of the Tuat smell the earth in paying homage to thee.

The uttermost parts of the earth bow before thee, and the limits of the skies entreat thee with supplications when they see thee.

The holy ones are overcome before thee, and all Egypt offers thanksgiving unto thee, Thy Majesty.

Thou art a shining Spirit-Body,

The governor of Spirit-Bodies,

Permanent is thy rank, established is thy rule.

Thou art the positive Sekhem of the Neteru,

Gracious is thy face, and beloved by him that sees it.

Thy fear is set in all the lands by reason of thy perfect love,

and they cry out to thy name making it the first of names,

and all people make offerings to thee.

Thou art the lord who art commemorated in heaven and upon earth.

Many are the cries which are made to thee

With one heart and voice Egypt raises cries of joy to thee.

From The Book of Coming Forth by Day (The Book of the Dead)

Adorations to RA/RAAT

DUA RA DUA RAAT
We thank you for loving us eternally
We thank you for healing us eternally
DUA RA DUA RAAT
We thank you for giving eternally
We thank you for guiding us eternally
DUA RA DUA RAAT
We thank you for shining eternally
We thank you for sharing eternally
DUA RA DUA RAAT
We thank you for feeding us eternally
We thank you for warming us eternally
DUA RA DUA RAAT

By Kajara Nebthet

Restore my eye, O DJEHUTI

Restore my eye, O DJEHUTI
Messenger of wisdom
Apply Hekau to my eye
Cause me to remember my essential nature
and glory
Provide me with the strength and will needed to
Overthrow duality, overthrow the illusions
of the third dimension
Assist me in directing my eye
Against evil and unrighteousness
Help me to know the immortal and perfect nature
of my soul
The Sahu is my goal, my aspiration
Assist me in unifying and deifying
My mental and spiritual aspects

Restore my eye, O DJEHUTI
Messenger of wisdom
Restore my eye!

The Sahu—The spiritual body in which the immortal spiritual soul (Khu) and heart-soul (Ba) dwells. When integrated, one becomes Godlike—liberated, while still alive.

By Mut Shat Shemsut

Adorations to MAAT

MAAT ankhu MAAT
MAAT nebuten
Cha hena MAAT
Ankh hena MAAT
Ha sema MAAT
MAAT her ten
Dua MAAT nebuten

Translation

MAAT is the source of life
MAAT is everywhere you are
Rise in the morning with MAAT
Live with MAAT
Let every limb join with MAAT
MAAT is who you are deep down
Adorations to Goddess MAAT
who is everywhere you are

From the Berlin papyrus
Submitted by Mut Shat Shemsut

A Hymn to MAAT

Praised even by the Gods and Goddesses
MAAT is the personification of the stability of the universe
I rise with MAAT every day
And speak or present the 42 utterances

MAAT is ever on my mind, guiding my actions
Elevating my thoughts and words
The gift of MAAT is mental peace and a purity of heart
MAAT is breath to my nostrils

MAAT is ever on my mind as I seek out
Find, and walk a path of righteousness
I shine light along the way inviting others to see
Feel the bliss that comes with balance and harmony

Through MAAT I travel to my very own self
Transcending the universe of duality
I fly to the cosmic consciousness within
I fly to my true nature, I fly to Truth.

By Mut Shat Shemsut

Hymn to AUSET

I Awaken to Divine Wisdom
I wake within the primordial waters
I am thrust into the light of the physical world
I cry a cry for now I am awake
I breathe SHU SHU SHU SHU
I drink TEFNUT TEFNUT TEFNUT TEFNUT
A lapis is placed on my crown
and silver is placed around my neck
Rehkit (wisdom) is whispered in my ear
She holds me in her arms
and keeps the darkness away
I am safe with she who gave me life.

By Ethereal-Chanie (Netret Pekh Ramu)

INVOCATION FOR GUIDANCE

GREAT MOTHER AUSET

Hold me in your arms

I am your child and I am in need of healing

Protect me from the evil in this world

Shine your light within me

Allow me to drink from your bosom

Nourish me with you wisdom

AUSET it is you that lights the darkness

It is you born from the darkness in which all creation exists

Great one of Heka

Eye of RA

Daughter of NUT and GEB

She who assembled the body of AUSAR

I call on you to show me the way as I am lost

Speak to me now!

As you hold me and protect me like mother and child

Show me the way out of this situation (name situation)

I ask that you hear my voice and remove the fog from my life

Bring peace into my life once again

DUA AUSET

By Ethereal-Chanie (Netret Pekh Ramu)

Hymn to HERU

O HERU
Mighty One
Whose power vanquished the enemy of his father
I come to ask that you guide me on this journey.
Walk with me Mighty One
Help me to overcome my enemies.
Give me wisdom and discernment in my decisions.
Let me speak, walk and act with higher consciousness.
Let me be aware of what is going on around me.
Let me find solutions to my problems
I honor you great one
And I thank you
DUA HERU
DUA NTR

By Kajara Nia Yaa Nebthet

Invocation for Protection

Oh SEKHMET,
source of strength and mercy,
lady of the burning sands,
SEKHMET, Mistress of Terror
May no enemy find me,
May no Harm approach me,
Your sacred fire surrounds me,
No evil can withstand Your eye.
Oh SEKHMET
Overcomer of all enemies,
Place your protective mantle around me,
help me remain steadfast and resolute in front of my enemies.
Shield and defend me and my loved ones from the ravages of fear and anxiety.
Oh SEKHMET,
I praise and honor you for your protection.

Sa Sekhem Sahu
TUA SEKHMET
TUA NTR

By Sherihat Ampesh Re

Adorations to SEKHMET

Tunnua SEKHMET Ntrt

Unen a em pet ari

Utu na em Het Ka Ptah

Rek a em aba

Sekhem a em haita

Sekhem a em aaui a

Sekhem a em ret a

Sekhem a em arit

Merit k a an qena tu

Ba a er kata her sbau nu

Amentet em aq a

Em Htp

Pert em Htp

Translation

May the Goddess SEKHMET raise me, and lift me up.

Let me ascend into heaven, let that which I command be performed in Het-ka-Ptah.

I know how to use my heart.

I am master of my heart.

I am master of my hands and arms.

I am master of my legs.

I have the power to do that which my KA desires to do.

My Heart-soul shall not be kept a prisoner in my body at the gates of Amentet

When I would go in in peace and come forth in peace.

from the Book of Coming Forth by Day

Hymn to the Great Mothers of Kemet

Anech Hrauk Iuasse-t Mut Ur eta em

Duba ren

Mut ur en ankh

Eta em septet en NUT

Eta e sheshet a en ankh

Eta em hetep en Meri

Eta em HET HERU

Eta em NEBTHET

Eta em MAAT en taui

Eta em udja en Irit en shekhem

Tuau Maa ab ani tu

Translation

Honor to the Great Mother the throne who comes as

Ten thousand names

Great Mother of Life

Who comes as stars of heaven

Who comes as the mysteries of the tree of life

Who comes as peace and love

Who comes as the house of light

Who comes as the lady of the constellation of houses

Who comes as Mother on heaven and earth

Who comes as the (Aje) the primordial serpent of light who gives us spiritual power.

Thank you Ma, my heart belongs to you

Submitted by Ayele Kumari

THE SEVEN HET-HERAS AT TANTERA (Dendera)

We beat the drum for your spirit

We dance for your majesty

We raise high your image to the heights of heaven

It is you who are the Lady of the Sekhem (power) and the most menet (sacred jewelry)

The Lady of the sistrum (divine rattle)

Music is made by your ka (spirit)

We honor your majesty, making offerings from sunset to dawn

It is you who are:

The lady of joyful music.

The lady of the iab dance

The lady of sounding the sistrum

The lady of singers

The lady of the kheb dance

The lady of weaving garlands

The lady of beauty

The lady of the keskes dance

The Great Seshat

The lady over the Neteru

When Your two eyes open as the sun and the moon,

Our hearts rejoice in seeing the light

It is you who are the lady of the dance wreaths

The lady of those who are drunk with joy

We do not dance and drum for any other

We devote ourselves to your divine spirit alone.

Submitted by Ayele Kumari

Heka for Healing

Dua SEKHMET,
Dua AUSET
Ari Mes
Ankh Udja Seneb

Translation

Adorations to Goddess SEKHMET
Adorations to Goddess ASET
Do for this child
Life, Vitality and Health

By Tchiya Amet

HYMN FOR PROTECTION

Anedj-Rak NEBT-HET,

Mistress and Head of the House;

none may enter unless they come thru you.

You sit at the threshold of the house of Ra and usher in love, peace, and joy.

Benevolent Goddess giver of life and abundance,

you are my guide and comfort in times of trial.

You lift me out of darkness that I may feel the strength and light of Ra.

Great Goddess, I give thanks to you;

Proctectress of women and children.

I pray thee, protect me and my household from the wicked plots and plans of those who wish to do harm against us.

Balance the scales of MAAT

so that all the traps and arrows of my oppressors be turned against them.

Anedj-Rak NEBT-HET

Dua RA

Dua NEBT-HET

ASÉ ASÉ ASÉ

By Aqseshsha Asu-At

Heka for Enlightenment

Nuk pu nuk khu

Ami khu quemen

Kheperu em NTR hau

Nuk ua em ennu

En pu ami khu

AMEN RE

TUA NTR

ANKH UDJA SENEB

Translation

I am a shining being and a dweller in light.

I have been created and come from the limbs of NTR.

I am one of those light beings dwelling in the light of Amen RA.

Adorations to The Most High.

Life Prosperity Good Health

Submitted by Kajara Nia Yaa Nebthet

Kemetic Proverbs

THE WAY TO IMMORTALITY:

"NETER sheds light on they who shake the clouds of Error from their soul, and sight the brilliancy of TRUTH, mingling themselves with the ALL-sense of the Divine Intelligence, through LOVE of which they win their freedom from that part over which TRANSFORMATION rules, and has the seed of the assurance of future Deathlessness implanted in him. This, then, is how the good will differ from the bad."

"If you seek NETER (GOD), you seek for the beautiful. One is the path that leads unto NETER (GOD)–Devotion *joined* with Gnosis."

"For the ill of ignorance does pour over all the earth and overwhelm the SOUL that's battened down w/in the flesh, preventing it from finding salvation."

Submitted by Barbara Holmes

KEMETIC PROVERBS

KNOW THYSELF

"The purpose of all human life is to achieve a state of consciousness apart from bodily concerns."

"Man is to become GOD-like through a life of virtue and the cultivation of the spirit through scientific knowledge, practice, and bodily discipline."

"To FREE the SPIRIT, CONTROL the senses; the reward will be a clear INSIGHT."

"Make your life the subject of intense inquiry, in this way you will discover its goal, direction, and destiny."

Submitted by Barbara Holmes

Chants for Sekhem

Chant #1

This chant stimulates and helps with building your psychic self defense.

SEKHMET Erta Na Hekau Apen SEKHMET

Translation

May I be given the words of power of SEKHMET

Repeat this chant up to 19 times in the morning before you set off into the outside world.

Chant #2

Yaa SEKHMET (inhale deep exhale saying)
Yaa SEKHMET (inhale deep exhale saying)
Yaa SEKHMET

It is good to do this chant to open the solar plexus, igniting the inner fire, getting your healing power flowing and building your shield of protection.

It is good to do deep breaths, expanding the stomach exhaling through the mouth, escalating to fire breaths, Inhale deep breaths and exhale Yaa SEKHMET.

by Sherihat Ampesh Re

Invocations to ORISHA

The Great Forces of West Afrika

THE ORISHA

The Orisha are the powerful deities of the Yoruba people of Nigeria, West Africa. There are hundreds of Orisha. We have listed some of the Orisha and their attributes.

OBATALA is the King of the White Cloth, wisdom, patience

ELEGBA/ESU is the divine messenger, gatekeeper, owner of power

OGUN is the ironsmith, metal work, iron, strength, war

OCHOOSI is the great hunter, woodsman

SANGO is the great King, warrior, justice, balance

YEMAYA is the great Mother, protector, nurturer

OSUN is Mother of love, beauty, joy, wealth

OYA is the Mother of change, storms, dreams

ORI is the spirit of head, high destiny, higher self

ELA is the spirit of white light, holy spirit

OLOKUN is the owner of the ocean, mysteries

EGUN are ancestral spirits

Ifa Morning Prayer

Opé ni fún OLÓRUN.
Ìbà OLÓDÙMARÈ.
Mó jí lòní.
Mo wo'gun mérin ayé.
Ìbà'se ilà Oòrùn.
Ìbà'se iwò Oòrun,
Ìbà'se Aríwá.
Ìbà'se Gúúsù..
Ìbà Òrun Òkè.
Ìbà Atíwò Òrun.
Ìbà Egún, Egúngún kiki egúngún,
Ìbà Orí,
Ìbà Orí inú.
Ìbà Ìponrí ti ò wa'l'Òrun.
Ìbà ÈSÙ, Èsù Òdàrà, Èsù, lanlu ogirioko. Okunrin orí ita.
Ìbà ÒSÓÒSÌ ode mátá.
Ìbà ÒGÚN awo, olumaki, Oníle kángu - kángu Òrun.
Ìbà OBÀTÁLÀ, Òrìsà Òséré Igbó. Oni kùtúkùtú awo òwúrò, Ikù iké, Ori tutu
Ìbà OLÓKUN à - sòrò - dayò.
Ìbà YEMOJA Olúgbé - rere.
Ìbà OSUN oloriya igún aréwa obirin.
Ìbà ÒLUKÓSÓ aira, bàmbí omo arigbà según.
Ìbà Àjáláiyé Àjàlórun OYA Olúwèkù.
Ìbà Ìbejì orò.
Ibà Ajé - ògúngúlùsò Olámbo yeye aiyé.

ÒRÚNMÌLÀ Elérì ìpín, ibikeji Olodumare. A- je - je - OGUN obiriti - a - p'ijo - iku da.

Ìbà Awòn Ìyáàmi, Alágogo èsìwù á p'oni a hangun alakiki oru.

Ase'

Translation

Thanks to the Owner of the Realm Heaven

I honor the Creator

I awake today.

I behold the Four Corners of the World.

I honor the power of the East.

I honor the power of the West.

I honor the power of the North.

I honor the power of the South.

I respect the Invisible Realm of the Mountains.

I respect all things that live in the Invisible Realm.

Praise to the mediums of the Ancestors

I respect the Spirit of Consciousness.

I respect the Spirit of the Inner Self.

I respect the Spirit of the higher self who lives in the Invisible Realm of the Ancestors.

I respect the Divine Messenger, Divine Messenger of Transformation, Divine Messenger speak with power. Man of the crossroads.

I respect the Spirit of the Tracker, Owner of the Mystery of Spotted Medicine.

I respect the Mystery of the Spirit of Iron, Spirit of strength and courage, the owner of innumerable homes in the Realm of the Ancestors.

I respect the Spirit of the King of White cloth who is praised at the Sacred Grove. Owner of the Ancient Mystery of the White Cloth, the Spirit Who is praised on the sacred day of the Forest, Guardian of those with physical disabilities. Keep my head cool.

I respect the Mystery of the Spirit of Iron, Spirit of strength and courage, the owner of innumerable homes in the Realm of the Ancestors.

I respect the Spirit of the King of White Cloth who is praised at the Sacred Grove. Owner of the Ancient Mystery of the White Cloth, the Spirit

I respect the Spirit of the Ocean, the one who makes things prosper.

I respect the Mother of Fishes, the Giver of Good Things.

I respect the Spirit of the River, owner of the hair comb for beautiful women.

I respect the King who does not die the Child of the Thunderstone.

I respect the Winds of Earth, the Winds of the Invisible Realm of the Ancestors, the Spirit of the Wind is the one who guides the mediums of the Ancestors.

I respect the Transforming power of the Spirit of the Twins.

I respect the Spirits of Wealth and Good Fortune, honor is coming to the Mothers of the Earth.

Spirit of Destiny, Witness to Creation, second only to the Creator. He who has the medicine to overcome Death.

I respect the Society of Wise Women, the Mothers, the White Bird of Power is the Source of their Medicine.

Let it be done.

Submitted by Ayele Kumari

Chant for Protection

Ko si iku
Ko si ano
Ko si ejo
Ko si ofo
Ko si ona
Ko si akoba
Ko si fitibo
Ko si ina
Ko si epe
Ko si oran
Ko si ashelu
Ko si egba
Ko si ewan
Ko si eshe

Fun mi ni Alafia
Fun mi ni tutu
Fun mi ni ilera
Fun mi ni ifa
Fun mi ni ire
Fun mi ni ire aiku
Fun mi ni irea arat'orunwa
Fun mi ni ire elese O'sa
Fun mi ni ire aiye
Fun mi ni l'owo
Fun mi ni ire obirin

Fun mi ni ire dedewat'olokun

Fun mi ni ire omo

Fun mi ni ire okunrin

Fun mi ni ire owo

Fun mi I ire aburo

Fun mi ni ire elese abure

Fun mi ni ire eleda

Fun mi ni ire elese egun

Translation

Keep away death

Keep away sickness

Keep away tragedy

Keep away sudden wrong, disturbance, embarrassment, losses, setbacks, witchcraft

Keep away vicissitude, upset, stumble

Keep away revolution

Keep away small obstacles

Keep away nervous disorders

Keep away curses

Keep away big trouble

Keep away injustice

Keep away paralysis

Keep away prison

Keep away all else that is bad

May I receive peace

May I receive clarity and freshness

May I receive stable home

May I receive spiritual elevation

May I receive grace

May I receive good by way of the dead

May I receive good from the heavens

May I receive good from the feet of the Orisha

May I receive good in this world

May I receive good by my own hands

May I receive good by way of a woman

May I receive good from the sea

May I receive good by way of a child

May I receive good by way of a man

May I receive good by way of money

May I receive good by way of an elderly person

May I receive good by way of a brother/friend

May I receive good by way of your own head

May I receive good by way of a dead person

Our Yoruba ancestors would add these chants to their prayers for extra power and protection. This is said everyday and acts like a shield.

Submitted by Kajara Nia Yaa Nebthet

Oriki

Oriki are praise songs or poems of the Yoruba people of West Afrika. They are sung or recited to pay honor to an individual, often during communal ceremonies. They include family history, accomplishments, admirations and warnings. There are some that are unique and created for a specific individual or family. There are some that are used internationally and have been carried from West Africa to countries all over the world.

The words in the oriki are used to call the Ori, the higher consciousness or the head. When a child is born in Yorubaland, an oriki is created for them. It is sung throughout the person's life to help them remember their family and culture, and to give strength to the individual during challenging times. It is also sung to strengthen family ties. Praise names and stories are often used in oriki. Also, they usually highlight one's achievements and might.

There are many types of oriki: oriki for The Creator, oriki for Orisha, oriki for kings or chiefs, oriki for towns, oriki for families, etc. In fact it is said that all living things have oriki.

We have included, here, some powerful oriki for the Orisha which can be used to invoke their presence.

ORIKI ELA

Ifá rò wá o.
ÈLÀ rò wá o o.
Bí ò n be lápá òkun.
Kó rò moo bo.
Bí ò n be ní wánrán oojúmo. Ase.
ÈLÀ rò, . ÈLÀ rò, ÈLÀ rò, ÈLÀ rò
Ase

Translation

Ifa please descend, Spirit of purity be present.
If you are at the ocean please come.
If you are in mid lagoon, please come.
Even if you are at wanran in the east, please come.
Holy Spirit descend, Holy Spirit descend, Holy Spirit descend, Holy Spirit descend…….
Let it be done.

Submitted by Ayele Kumari

Oriki ESU

ESU pele o,

Okaramaho, Ayarabata-awo-'le-oja,

Oyinsese, Segiiri-alagbaja,

Olofin-apeka'lu, Amonisegun-mapo.

ESU, Ori mi ma je Nkomo o.
ESU, Ba nse ki imo.
ESU, K'eru o Ba onimimi.
ESU, fun mi foo ase, mo pele Orisha.
ESU, Alayiki a juba.
Ase

Translation

Divine messenger, I call you by your names of praise.

Divine messenger, guide my head towards the path of destiny.

Divine messenger, I honor your deep wisdom.

Divine messenger find a place for my sorrows.

Divine messenger give me the words of power so that I might greet the Forces of Nature.

Divine Messenger, we pay our respects by dancing in a circle.

Ase.

Submitted by Deborah Gear

Oriki ELEGBA

ELEGBA ma ni ko.

ELEGBA, ma ya ko.

ELEGBA, f'ohun tire sile.

ELEGBA ohun olohun ni I a wa kiri.

Ase.

Translation

The owner of Power causes confrontation.
Owner of Power do not confront me.
The Owner Of Power has the voice of power.
The Divine Messenger has a voice that can be heard throughout the universe.
Ase.

Submitted by Deborah Adel'oni Gear

Oriki OGUN

OGUN okunrin OGUN ato polowo iku

Eni tii somo eniyan dolola

En OGUN ko gbe bi eni ti ko robi sebo

Gbigbe ni o gbe mi bi oti gbe

Akinoro ti o fi kole ola

OGUN awoo alaka aye Osanyin imole

Egbe lehin eni a nda loro

OGUN gbe mi o

Ase

Translation

Spirit of Iron, the powerful one, sufficiently great to avert death.

One who makes human prosperous.

One who is not enriched by the Spirit of Iron will find it difficult to get sacrificial kola nut.

Spirit of Iron enriches me as you enriched Akinro and made him an eminent man.

Spirit of Iron, the powerful one, the strong one of the Earth, the great one of the other world.

The protector of those who are being injured.

Spirit of Iron support me.

Let it be so

Submitted by Kajara Nia Yaa Nebthet

ORIKI OCHOOSI

Ibo OCHOOSI

Iba olog'arare

Iba Onibebe

Iba Osolokere

Ode ata mata se

Agbani nijo to buru

Oni ode gan fi di ja

Ajuba

Ase

Translation

I praise the spirit of the tracker

I praise the Master of Himself

I praise the Owner of the River bank

I praise the Magician of the forest hunter who never misses

Wise spirit who offers many blessings

Owner of the parrot that guides me to overcome fear

I salute you

Let it be so

Submitted by Kajara Nia Yaa Nebthet

ORIKI OBATALA

Iba OBATALA,
Iba Oba Igbo,
Iba Oba, N'le ifon,
O fi koko ala rumo,
Orisha ni ma sin.
Orisha ni ma sin Orisha ni ma sin.
OBATALA o su n'nu ala.
OBATALA o tinu ala dide.
A-di-ni bout ri, mojuba.
Ase.

Translation

Praise to the chief of the white cloth.
Praise to the chief of the sacred grove.
Praise to the chief of Heaven, I salute the owner of white cloth.
It is the owner of white light that I serve.
Chief of the white cloth sleeps in white.
Chief of the white cloth awakes in white.
Chief of the white cloth gets up in white.
He who creates at will, I thank you.
May it be so.

Submitted by Deborah Adel'oni Gear

ORIKI OLOKUN

OLOKUN Ajikolu Oba ninu omi
Emila lale odo
Bojumo bamo, OLOKUN Alugbudu
Bojumo bamo OLOKUN Alugbadu
Asan rere kan aye
Oosa tio lowo
Oosa tio lese
Ogbewon sanle yakata
Dakun mo gbemi sanle ni temi
Tuntun ni o tunmi lori se
Abiyamo tin yomo re lofin

Translation

OLOKUN, the great that everyone greets everyday, the King of all water.
The mighty one inside the river.
When the day comes, OLOKUN will beat quietly.
When the day comes, OLOKUN will beat loudly.
The one that flows and covers the earth.
The Orisa with no hands.
The Orisa with no legs.
And yet, he still carries them and smacks them down easily
Please don't smack me down
Remold and renew is what you should do to my Ori
The great mother that removes her children from a great problem

By Elebuibon Awoyinfa Abereifa

ORIKI YEMAYA

Iba YEMAYA yalode

Agbe ni igbe re ki YEMAYA

Ibekeji odo

YEMAYA pele o

YEMAYA pele o

YEMAYA pele o

Ni igba meta

YEMAYA ni ka le

Oro ti ase fun YEMAYA

ni awon omo re was se fun oyi o

YEMAYA ba me

A juba

Ase

Translation

I respect the Mother of Fishes, Queen of the Sea

It is the bird who delivers abundance to the Mother of fishes, Goddess of the Sea

Mother of Fishes I greet you

Mother of Fishes I greet you

Mother of Fishes I greet you

The power of transformation that comes from the Mother of Fishes is beyond understanding.

Mother of fishes save me

I give praise

Let it be so

Submitted by Kajara Nia Yaa Nebthet

ORIKI SANGO

Ibe se Oba ko Baba SANGO
Aiya ki if'odo
Aiya ki if'odo
SANGO ba mi o
K'aiya mi ma ja mo
K'eru ma ba me mo o
A juba o
Ase – to

Translation

I respect the chief who does not die
The father of lightning
The mortar does not know fear
The grindstone does not know fear
Spirit of lightning save me
Let me no longer experience fear
Let me never know fear
I give thanks
May it be so

Submitted by Kajara Nia Yaa Nebthet

ORIKI OSUN

Ore Yeye O!

Ore Yeye O!

Ore yeye moroo!

Oro Yeye, O soroo

Ogidi omi

Iyaa wa maagbo onile agodi

Iyaa Ijesa pele aloyinlorun

Kaare!

Lule O! Omi O!

Ota O! Edan O!

Eri O! Agba O!

Translation

Blessings my mother

Blessings my mother

Blessings my mother the one with wealth!

My mother's matter is a serious one

The strong water

Our mother be hearing the one with Agodi House

The mother of Ijesa be hearing, the one that have honey in her pot

How are you? The one with enough

Water O! Pebbles O!

Iron statue O! bracelets O!

River O! Barrels O!

Submitted by Awoyinfa Elebuibon, son of Araba of Osgbo, Ifayemi Elebuibon

ORIKI OYA

OYA yeba Iya mesa OYA
Orun afefe Iku lele bioke
Auaba gbogbo le ya obinrin
Ogo mi ano gbogbo gun
Orisa mi ayaba
OYA ewa OYAnsa
Ase

Translation

Spirit of the Wind
Senior Mother of Oyo
Heaven's wind bring down the ancestors
Queen of All women
Always protect me with your strong medicine
My guardian spirit is the Queen
Spirit of the wind and Mother of Nine
May it be so

Submitted by Kajara Nia Yaa Nebthet

Oriki for Primordial Mothers

Nwon ba nkorin bayi pe
Iya kere e mo ohun mi o
IYAMI OSONRONGA, gbogbo ohun ti mba nwi
Ogbo lo ni e mda gbo dandan
IYAMI OSORONGA, e mo ohun mi o
IYAMI OSORONGA, igba l o ni ki e mda gba
IYAMI OSORONGA, e mo ohun mi o
IYAMI OSORONGA, oro ti okete ba le so Ni le gbo dandan
IYAMI OSORONGA, e mo ohun mi o
IYAMI OSORONGA, gbogbo ohun ti mba ti nwi, ni ko mda se
IYAMI OSORONGA, mo ohun mi o
Ase

Translation

Petite mother you will know my voice
IYAMI OSORONGA (My mother the sorceress) every word that I speak
The ogbo leaf has said that you will understand it absolutely
IYAMI OSORONGA, you will know my voice
IYAMI OSORONGA, the calabash says that you will take it
IYAMI OSORONGA, you will know my voice
IYAMI OSORONGA, the word that the okete rat speaks to the earth
The Earth will hear it absolutely
IYAMI OSORONGA, you will know my voice
IYAMI OSORONGA, everything that I say, you will do
IYAMI OSORONGA, you will know my voice.
Ase O!

EAST, SOUTH, NORTH OR WEST, THE GREAT MOTHER IS THE FOUNDATION!

By Awo Fategbe Fatunmbi

ORIKI EGUN

Egungun wa yana wa neni
Je wa memu
Egungun Baba Iya wa o
Je wa gb'obi pa
Egungun wa yana wa
Ase

Translation

Ancestors please call on us today
And drink our palm wine
Ancestors, Fathers and Mothers please come
So that you may accept offerings
And split the kola nut
Ancestors please come
Let it be so

Submitted by Kajara Nia Yaa Nebthet

Oriki Ori

Orí san mi. Orí san mi.
Orí san igede. Orí san igede.
Orí otan san mi ki nni owo lowo.
Orí otan san mi ki nbimo le mio.
Orí oto san mi ki nni aya.
Orí oto san mi ki nkole mole.
Orí san mi o. Orí san mi o. Orí san mi o.
Oloma ajiki, ìwá ni mope.
A<u>se</u>.

Translation

Inner spirit guide me. Inner Spirit Guide me. Inner Spirit support me. Inner Spirit support me.

Inner Spirit support my abundance.

Inner Spirit support my future children

Inner Spirit support my relatiionships.

Inner Spirit protect my house.

Inner Spirit guide me. Inner Spirit guide me. Inner Spirit guide me.

Protector of Children and character.

Let it be done.

Submitted by Ayele Kumari

Adoration to OYA

OYA! She who comes in the night and is cloaked in darkness yet is as vibrant as the sun.

You are the wind, the tempetuous storm coming to clear the way and destroy all that is not for my highest good.

None may cross me unless they cross you; my defender and protector.

Great Mother, to you no detail is too small when it comes to your children.

You right the slightest to the grandest offense and to you I give praise and join in your victory dance.

Invincible one, you are the perfect companion for you are no stranger to war.

You keep my path clear that I may not stumble.

Compassionate one, you are the opener of the way and the embodiment of righteous anger.

With a twirl of your war-torn skirt, you usher in the winds of change. You are the air that I breathe and I fill my lungs to receive your healing essence.

Iya Yansah, the great Mother of nine! OYA, how you care for your children in their time of need!

To you I give thanks, and to you all praises and adoration are due!

Asé

By Aqseshsha Asu-At

Invocation for YEMAYA

My womb is the womb of creation

I am the ocean and the 7 seas

My children are the lightning and the tornado

I have the power to swallow the land and bring creation to my feet

I am forever ready to battle those who cross me

I am the moon who moves the waves

I am the power who keeps destruction away

My children are the rivers, creeks and rain.

For I am the water running through the planet like blood in the veins.

I am the Goddess of the oceans

Mother of the seas

I am adorned with pearls, shells and cowrie

I will come when you call me

So listen to your heart to hear my voice or a shell to your ear is just as good

I will wash you with my essence to purify your soul

As water is spirit worth more than gold

By Ethereal-Chanie (Netret Pekh Ramu)

CHANT TO ORI

Ori above
Ori before
Ori my head please adorn
Ori my guide
Ori my eyes
Ori with you my duty lies
Ori my shield
and protecting force
Ori connect me with the Source
Ori from you my blessings flow
I will not be moved til I hear your voice
Tutu Ori, Ori wu
Ori wu, Ori wu, Ori wu
Asé

Submitted by *Aqseshsha Asu-At*

PROPITATIONS TO ORI

From the Yoruba tradition

Yoruba Proverb:

It is the path of my Ori
(my spirit/that direct connection to Divine Source)
that I'm following, it is the errand of my Ancestors that I'm running

These propitiations were taught to Ifadunke Olayemi using the system of Yoruba Kabbalah

by Babalawo Modupe Opeola from Ile-Ife, Nigeria, West Africa.

Sharing of this knowledge has been blessed and sanctioned with his permission granted, March 9, 2014.

ORI CHANT FOR STABILITY, Otura Ofun

Otura funfun Awo Ori
Difa fun Ori
Ori nsunkun alainibudo
Ebo ni won ni ko waa se
O gb' ebo, o ru'bo
Ori je n nibudo
Ori je n nibudo gbayi o

Translation

Otura funfun, the White Otura, the Awo of Ori
He cast Ifa for Ori
When weeping that he had no stability in life
He was advised to offer Ebo
He complied
Ori, please let me have stability
My destiny, let me have stability this time around

My head do my will 3X
Ase 3X
Amen Ra, MAAT

Ori Wu
Chant while moving the palms away from the head, like expanding 3X

When performing the chant, sit on the floor with your feet forward legs uncrossed, place the palms of your hands flat on your head just above your ears.

Chant to Ori

We need to adore the head

Adore the head and not adore the medicine

To adore the medicine is not to adore the head

OOGUN (medicine) is the day of sadness and Ori is for all days

My Ori it is you

If I have children on earth, it is my Ori to whom I will give my praise.

My Ori it is you

You who gives blessings to your devotee more quickly than all the other Gods.

My Ori it is you.

No God bless a man without the consent of his Ori

My Ori it is you

Ori I hail you, you who allows children to be born alive.

A person's whose sacrifice is accepted by his own Ori shall rejoice exceedingly.

Perform while sitting on the floor, legs in front of the body uncrossed. Palms of hands over the ears.

Then address Ori as your fortune, your protection continue with a specific request.

Ashe 3x

AMEN RA, MAAT

My head do my will 3x

Ori Wu! 3x while moving the hands from the head.

Ori Propitation 3

The Yoruba Kabbalah cult (created before Jewish Kabbalah) uses the power of Pyramids and Circles.

To propitiate to Ori, draw a circle with either white chalk or efun.

Place a small fire proof dish in the center of the circle next to a pyramid. Pour gin (preferably high proof).

Use obi abata (four lobe obi) as the medium for divination. Light the gin, place the obi in your left hand, then make a fist.

Use your right hand to touch the ground in front of the flame. Use the right hand to slap the left hand 3x while saying

Ile mo pe (earth I'm calling on you)

Eti bre mo pe Ori 3x (Ori I'm calling on you)

Break the obi open.

Ask if Ori has arrived, then cast the obi until the answer is yes. When the four pieces are either all up; two up, two down; or all four down,

then proceed to make your prayer with your face over the flame and your hands cupping the left and right of your face.

Before the flame is out, make your prayer, ask if your prayer was accepted using the obi.

Ask where the obi goes. For example, stay in the circle, to the crossroads, near fresh water, near salt water, in the woods, near a tree, etc.

Pray until flame is out. When cool, drink. Note color of flame and any images. For example, white flame is purifying. Very effective for communicating with any Orisha through the circle

ORI PROPITATION 4

Supplies Needed
Glass of Cool Water
Obi Abata 4 or 5 lobe washed in cool water
White plate

Place the small glass of water on the floor.
Pour libation to call in the spirits
Hold the obi in your dominate hand while reciting

OLODUMARE, let my mind ascend onto thee for information and my soul for guidance - 7 times

Touch your forehead and chest three times.

Place the obi in your left hand then form a fist. Use your right hand to touch the ground in front of the glass while saying, Ile mo pe, 3 times then slap the top of the left hand.

Perform this step three times. then state

"*Etigbure Ori* I'm calling you" 3 times.

Open the obi and divide into four unique pieces. Remove the liver or (heart) from each lobe of obi. This system of obi divination requires either a four-five lobe obi, the fifth lobe, called ofuwa is placed on the shrine of ESU/ELEGBA after making a request. Holding the heart (liver) of obi in your hand then make a circle clockwise over your heart three times then throw into the glass of water.
Inquire to Ori by speaking your vibration directly into the obi, "Have you Arrived"?

Place the obi into your cupped hands, using a circular motion (clockwise) over the plate, then release the obi.

If the obi configuration is either all four up, all four down, or two up then you have received a yes.

State your singular request by framing in the positive. For example, Ori, will assist me in obtaining the best of employment in a good environment?
Next, inquire if Ori has a message.

Inquire if Ori sees ire or blessings. If the answer is no, then Ori sees a problem. Inquire if either the blessing (ire) or problem (ibi) is for yourself.
Determine by inquiring to Ori who the ire/problem is for? (Husband, children, etc)

Inquire if Ori will accept obi to either manifest the ire or terminate the problem . Inquire which Orisha will accept obi to either manifest the ire or terminate the problem.

Closing
Inquire if you may close? If not, then Ori has more messages or may require an offering of either cool water, obi, honey, gin etc. Any of these items may be offered to Ori by touching the forehead and chest three times. When permission is granted to close the session, promptly end the session.
Place the obi to the place (prescribed by Ori)

Place your palms above both sides of your head above your ears and say, my head do my will, three times. Then, Ori Wu while simultaneously extending the hands from your head 3 times.

Throw the water containing the heart/(liver) of obi on the ground in front of the place where the propitiation is taking place. Place the obi where instructed.

More prayers from Afrika

Akan Prayer

ODUMAKOMA nsa

ASASE YAA nsa

Kra nsa

Abasom nsa

Nsaman pa nsa, yedo mo ase

So moma yen nkwa,

Mma ahonya, odo ne ahoto monso yen mu daa daa

Nanso onipa busuyefo hara a

Ope se ade bone ba yen so no,

Nsoman pa yetwat no gu koran Saa onipa yi adi nkogu koraa!

Translation

Supreme Creator and Shining One,

We invoke your name,

Mother Earth who was created on Thursday,

We invoke your name.

Inner spirit, I invoke your name

Spirits of Nature, we invoke your name

Our venerable ancestors if I call one, I call all. We are grateful to you for granting us health, children, wealth love and peace.

We pray that you continue to protect us all.

But anyone who has evil thoughts against us in this family; the one who wishes that misfortunes happen to us, We pray that the person is completely overpowered!

Submitted by Kajara Nia Yaa Nebthet

Akan Libation

NANA NYAME, Otumfo
Me kyere wo nsuo, na menma wo nsuo
NANA NYAMEWAA, Obaatan Pa
Me kyere wo nsuo, na menma wo nsuo

Nana Nyankonton, bra nom nsuo
Nana Nyankopon, bra nom nsuo
Ye Nananom Nsamanfo, bra nom nsuo
Nana Aso Boade, bra nom nsuo
Nana Asiama Nyankopon Guahyia, bra nom nsuo
Asonafo pa, bra nom nsuo
Brietuofo pa, bra nom nsuo
Akanfo mmusuafo pa, bra nom nsuo
Abibifo Nsamanfo pa, bra nom nsuo
Nana Asaase Afua, bra nom nsuo
Nana Asaase Yaa, bra nom nsuo
Nana Awusi, bra nom nsuo
Nana Yaw, bra nom nsuo
Nana Bosom Afram ye ntoro, bra nom nsuo
Nananom Abosom nyinaa Nyamewaa-Nyame mma, bra nom nsuo

Yesre wo, gye aforebode
Yoooo.

Translation

*God, All Powerful One
I show you this drink, but I do not attempt to offer it to you
Goddess, our Good and Gracious Mother
I show you this drink, but I do not attempt to offer it to you
Creatress of the Universe, come, accept this drink
Creator of the Universe, accept this drink
Our Honorable Ancestresses and Ancestors, accept this drink
Great Spirit-Mother of the Asona Clan, accept this drink
Great Spirit-Mother of the Brietuo Clan, accept this drink
Good Ancestresses and Ancestors of the Asona Clan, accept this drink
Good Ancestresses and Ancestors of the Brietuo Clan, accept this drink
Good Akan Ancestresses and Ancestors of all of the Clans, accept this drink
Good Afurakani/Afuraitkaitnit (African/Black) Ancestresses and Ancestors, accept this drink
Earth Mother Afua, accept this drink
Earth Mother Yaa, accept this drink
The God Awusi, accept this drink
The God Yaw, accept this drink
The God Afram, our ntoro, accept this drink
All of the Goddesses and Gods of Creation, the Children of the Great Goddess and Great God, accept this drink

We appeal to you, accept these offerings
Yoooo*

Submitted by Kwesi Ra Nehem Ptah Akhan

Prayer to Nzambi

MFUMU NZAMBI, Zulu kele na Nge
Kansi ke pesaka yo na bantu
Ebuna, kwisa nzambi na beno
Na nzila ya mimpeva ti mimpungu
Nzambi mpungu kangula bibobo na mono
Ibuna munoko na mono tatuba nkembo na Nge
Banzio yonso ya Nzambi
Pesa lukwikulu ya mvimba na beno
Kwlsa sadika mono

Translation

All Powerful God, the skies to you belong
And you have given the lands to the men
It is said the spirits come across to us
In order to guide us in good ways
All Powerful god open your eyes to me
And my mouth will proclaim your praise
All the powers of God
Grant the fullness to us of faith in you
And come to my aid

Submitted by Kajara Nia Yaa Nebthet

KONGO CHANT TO SIMBI SPIRITS

Simba Simbi

Say your name at the end of the chant
repeat over and over

Simbi are connected to water. This chant can be used to divert danger away from you.

KONGO CHANT FOR BREAKTHROUGH

Buka Mukati Yabuka Kuumbazi

No Translation ...

These are words of Power

Submitted by Ayele Kumari

Prayers from the Diaspora

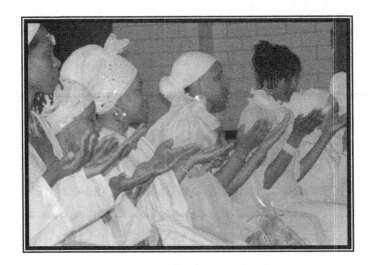

Prye Djo

Imado se O'angn nan d'lo
Oba Kosu miwa , lawe lawe
Imado se O'zangn nan d'lo
Oba kosu miwa, lawe, lawe
Nan lavil o'kane Kreyol mande chanjman.

Nu tut se sangn of sangn anba a se mwen
Nu tut se sangn o, sangn anba s se mwen
Dambala wedo, ayida wedo,
Nut tut se sagn o sangn anba a se mwen.atala,

atala atala na pral rele rele lwa yo, ago e
Atala atala na pral rele lwa yo ago e
Atala n'deja gen ason deja samaloge
Atala m'deja gen ason deja samaloge
Atalae mwen di e bonswa bonswa lwa'm yo

Minis o'dan sonnen dejevo a
Minis o'dan sonnen djevo a
Anko m'ungwe, an'ye djevo e
Ayi masa kule an'ye djevo e
O sala, salam sesgbo lovige, sala m'pungwe.

Misi yanvalu mwen ooooo
Micho mi yanvalu mwen

Misi yanvalu mwen Ooooo
Micho mi yanvalu mwern

Ta menfo, ta gwele misi yanvalu tone
Ta menfo, ta gwele, misi yanvalu tone
Misi laye koklo, koklo gidi adjalovi, Ooooo
Misi mi yanvalu mwen

Azaka mede, o yehvi danhomen
Azaka mede, o yehvi danhomen
Evi danhomen yehvi gweto e
Evi danhomen yehvi gweto e
Azaka mede o evi danhomen

Nou la, nouu la ogu o mwen die lolo ile
nour la do m'sanwo
Nou la, nour la ogu o
Mwen di e lolo ile, nou la do m'sanwo
Nou la, nou la ogu o
Nou la, nou la ogu o
Mwen di e lolo ile, nour la do m'sanwo

Pito pito se mwa leman e
Pito pito se mwa leman e
ma wele met ogu o,
ma wele met'feray o,
m'pa vle lwa yo tuye mwen

Sifle banbi kwalamen sifle, sifle o
Sifle banbi kwalamen sifle, sifle o
Sifle banbi kwalamen sifle wele lwa yo

Hu lwa wangol adje,
Dambala la flanbo kote out ye
Hu lwa wangol adje,
Dambala la flanbo kote ou ye
Gwanmesi laviej adje

Deye do nan ginen se pou lang yo
Deye do nan ginen se pou lang yo
Deye do nan ginen se pou lang yo
Afrika must be free !!!!

This prayer will invoke and honor the High Spirits of Vodun. Translation was not available. Sing instead of speaking this one.

Submitted by Kajara Nia Yaa Nebthet

Chippewa Prayer

O FATHER

Whose voice I hear in the winds and whose breath gives life to the world

Hear me

I am a man before you, one of your many children

I am small and weak

I need your strength and wisdom

Let me walk in beauty and make my eyes ever behold the red and purple sunsets

Make my hands respect the things you have made

Make my ears sharp to hear your voice

Make me wise so that I may know the things you have taught my people

The lessons you have hidden in every leaf and rock

I seek strength, Father

Not to be superior to my brothers but to be able to fight my worst enemy, Myself

Make me ever ready to come to you with clean hands and straight eye, so that when life fades as the fading sunset

My spirit may come to you without shame

By Tom S. Whitecloud

Mayan Prayer of the 7 Directions

From the East, House of Light, may wisdom dawn in us so we may see all things in clarity.

From the North, House of Night, may wisdom ripen in us so we may know all from within.

From the West, House of Transformation, may wisdom be transformed into right action, so we may do what must be done.

From the South, House of the Eternal Sun, may right action reap the harvest so we may enjoy the fruits of planetary being.

From Above, House of Heaven, may star people and ancestors be with us now.

From Below, House of Earth, may the heartbeat of her crystal core bless us with harmonies to end all war.

From the Center, Galactic Source, which is everywhere at once, may everything be known as the light of mutual love.

Oh Yum, Hunab Ku, Evam Maya E Ma Ho!

Oh Yum, Hunab Ku, Evam Maya E Ma Ho!

Oh Yum, Hunab Ku, Evam Maya E Ma Ho!

Translation

"Oh Mother, Source - the harmony of mind and nature
This phrase combines Mayan and Tibetan language.

Submitted by Qamarah Muhammed El Shamesh

Islamic Prayer

BISMILLAH ar-Rahman ar-Rahim.

Al-hamdu lillaahi Rabb al'aalamin.

Ar-Rahman ar-Rahim.

Maaliki Yawm-id-Din.

Iyyaaka na'budu wa iyyaaka nasta'in.

Ihdina-s-siraat al-mustaqim.

Siraat alladhina an'amta 'alayhim ghayr al-maghdubi 'alayhim wa laa adh-dhaalin.

Translation

In the name of Allah, the Beneficent, the Merciful;

All praise is due to Allah, the Lord of the worlds, the Beneficent, the Merciful,

Master of the day of requital.

Thee do we serve and Thee do we beseech for help.

Guide us on the right path of those upon whom Thou hast bestowed favors,

not of those upon whom Thy wrath is brought down, nor of those who go astray.

Amen.

Submitted by Qamarah Muhammed El Shamesh

Purification Prayer

P'hat Bambalasam
Nego Fram Bambalasam
Kumanyon Bambalasam
Nyon bambalasom
Kalakum Maangala

Translation

I purify with the power of blessedness.
No Energy can come to me and do me harm.
With these words I make all things pure,
Sacred for realizing my Godliness

The mantra, Phat removes negative energy.
Procedure:

    Place bowl of water with salt in center

    Draw energy from all around the room and throw it in the water to neutralize

    Snap fingers and move around head and in a fan like fashion to further facilitate the dispersing of stagnant energy.

    Discard water without touching

    Clean bowl and replace with fresh water with salt.

Submitted by Ayele Kumari

Sukhmani Sahib (Peace Lagoon)

GAURI SUKHMANI: GURU ARJUN
SLOK

Aad Guray Nameh.

Jagaad Guray Nameh.

Sat Guray Nameh.

Siree Guroo Dayv-ay Nameh

Translation

I bow to the primal Guru

I bow to the Guru of all ages.

I bow to the True Guru.

I bow to the great invisible Guru.

ASHTAPADI I

To the one who meditates on Him (Her) there
comes a perfect peace,
And all pain and sorrows depart.
Meditate on Him (Her), Who contains this universe,
Whose Holy Name is the whisper on the lips
Of the entire creation.
The Vedas, the Puranas and the Smiritis,
sustaining the purest truths,
Were created out of a portion of God's Name.
Into that heart which God has blessed with a hint of His
(Her) Name.

There comes a greatness beyond all praise.
To him (her) who seeks only to gain a sight of Thee
Is granted the grace to save all men (humanity);
Nanak prays, save me along with them!

This perfect peace is found in the nectar
of His (her) Name.
It is the Name of God that dwells in the hearts of His (Her) lovers:
Meditate upon it.

It is by meditating on the Lord that one
Is released from the bondage of rebirth,
One is freed from fear of pain or death,
and escapes the limitations of mortality.
His (Her) eneimies will keep away from him (her),
And he (she) will be safe from all harm.
His (Her) mind will be ever aware,
And will not be touched by fear or sorrow.
So meditate in the company of the holy,
For it is in loving the Lord that one gains
All His (Her) treasures, O Nanak

It is in meditating on the Name that one gains
All wealth of earthly goods, of mental
Powers and aesthetic pleasures.

*In the illumination gained from the thought
of Him (Her) is found all knowledge, all devotion
and the essence of all wisdom.
Meditation on the Lord is the true
contemplation, austerity and worship.
In contemplating Him (Her) one dissolves all
sense of duality and sees nothing
but the One everywhere.
By thinking of Him (her) one is truly bathed
in all waters of holiness,
And every action bears the purest fruits.
They alone meditate upon Him (Her) who are
blessed by the Lord; Nanak seeks to
touch their feet.*

*The repetition of the Holy Name is
the highest practice of all;
It has saved many a human soul.
By it the desires of the restless mind
are fulfilled,
And all knowledge is imparted to a man (woman).
To such a man (woman) death loses its terrors,
He (she) feels all his (her) hopes fulfilled,
His (Her) mind is cleansed of all impurities,
And his (her) heart is filled with the ambrosial Name.
The Lord lives on the tongue of His (Her) saints.*

*Nanak is a slave to those who
serve their Lord.*

*Only those who love the Name
experience that richness;
They alone are honorable.
They are accepted in the eyes of God (The Goddess);
And are the true rulers of mankind (humankind).
They who practice the Name depend
On none but the Lord,
And they are the masters of all.
They who practice the name live in joy,
And attain life everlasting.
He (She) alone meditates on the Name whom
The Goddess (The God) has blessed;
Nanak seeks the dust of such men's (women's) feet.*

*Such men (women) of God (The Goddess) perform
good deeds for others.
I am a sacrifice unto such a one!
His (Her) face emits a radiant glow,
And he (she) lives in a constant peace.
It is the repetition of the Name that is
the true self-discipline*

*By which one follows a path of righteousness,
And gains access to the manifold
sources of bliss.
Through the contemplation of the Name of
the Lord, one lives ever in His (Her) presence.
It is by the blessing of such holy men (women)
that the
mind is made wakeful both day and night
To the call of the Lord.
O Nanak, he (she) alone meditates on the Lord
whose destiny is perfect.*

*Through the contemplation of His (Her) Name a
man (woman) is assured success in all
undertakings,
And will never come to grief.
His (Her) tongue is busy with the praise of God (The
Goddess),
And his (her) mind is fixed on the steady vision.
Nothing can shake it;
Within blooms the lotus of the mind,
And the unstruck melody of the Word
resounds in his (her) ear.
Unspeakable is the peace that comes from
singing God's (The Goddess') Name.
Who sing it but those to whom God (The Goddess) is
kind?*

*O Nanak, if they would take me into the
safety of their fellowship!
By the remembrance of His (Her) Name,
a man (woman) becomes a saint.
It was the praise of His (Her) Name that inspired
the Vedas,
And inspired men (women) to be adepts, celibates
And men (women) of compassion.
The practice of The Name has turned obscure
men (women) into luminaries of the world.
It was for the glorification of the Name
that the world was made.
O, think of the Lord as the Cause of all Causes!
His (Her) name has brought all forms into being.
Himself (Herself) the Formless One lives in the
utterance of the Name.
Nanak, when by His (Her) grace He (She) imparts
this understanding to a man (woman)
He (She) learns to practice the Name though
the Guru.*

Insert—This prayer brings everlasting peace. It opens the heart to live in gratitude and steadies your spiritual discipline. It gives courage.

Submitted by Mut Shat Shemsut

Prayers for Libation

Pouring Libations

Libation is the act of pouring a liquid to call on or invoke our ancestors, spirit guide/s, deities, the elements (air, fire, water, earth) and other aspects of nature (rivers, streams etc). Libations are poured to acknowledge and to be acknowledged by our ancestors, spirit guide/s and deities. We pour libation to gain their attention and open a communication channel.

Water, alcohol, palm wine, wine, and soft drinks are liquids that can be used for libation. The choice of liquid is usually determined by the reason for pouring libation. Libation can be poured to call on ancestors for messages, protection, to open doors for an individual, for healing and much more. In addition, libations can be poured when calling on ancestors and spirit guides just to honor them.

For the purpose of this book we will focus on the basic principles of pouring libation with water.

A vessel is needed from which the libation will be poured as well as an appropriate vessel *into* which the libation will be poured. A calabash, wooden bowl, seashell, glass bowl or glass chalice is ideal. Use only natural material; do not use plastic or anything unnatural as it is important to stay connected to mother earth and the natural elements. It is best to pour the libation onto the ground. However, libation can be poured into a plant, or any of the vessels previously mentioned.

The person pouring the libation can also dip their fingers into the water and sprinkle it around themselves. If in a place where the libation can't be physically poured, and the person is comfortable with the act of pouring libation, the alternative is to drink the water instead.

Preparing the Space

In your personal space you can light a candle, burn some incense or spray some perfume to invite your ancestors. Use clean water such as spring water, purified water, rain, river, or ocean water. Use the highest quality water you have. Do not use tap water!

When you pour it is best that you have at least one knee on the ground. This is usually overlooked. However, ensure you have washed yourself and have fresh breath.

When calling on your ancestors only call on the ancestors who lived their lives in a righteous way. You will call on those who are connected to you by your bloodline and elevated ancestors who served the entire community (for example: Marcus Garvey and Harriet Tubman). Don't call on ancestors who committed suicide, committed murders, abused others, deceased children and so forth. If you are not sure ask a family member about the ancestor before calling on them.

When saying your libation prayer, try to use words from your African indigenous families as it will give strength to your prayer. You can call the names of both your paternal and maternal ancestors. If you don't know their names you can call your benevolent ancestors.

Do not rush when pouring libation, be sincere because your ancestors know your thoughts. Speak with truth and good intent. Talk to them as if they are in the room with you. Always thank them for their presence in your life. Finally, don't be afraid of your ancestors, spirit guide/s or deity. They are here to guide you in the physical realm. They will bring balance to your life.

The libations in this book will help you open the way and make a connection to your ancestors, spirit guide/s and deities.

By Ethereal-Chanie (Netret Pekh Ramu)

Prayer for Libation

DUA NTR

We give thanks and praises to the Creator of All Things, known by many names

We thank you for giving us this day.

We thank you for all things both great and small.

We give thanks to the elements

Air, Fire, Water, Earth

We give thanks to All Great Forces of Nature

We give thanks to our Great and Divine Spirit Guides

We give thanks to our Great and Noble Ancestors who watch over our family (say their names)

We give thanks to the Elevated Ancestors who worked to uplift our people (say their names)

We ask you to continue to walk with us

Bless this home and my family

Protect us from all hurt and harm

Let us treat and speak to each other with kindness.

Let us use our time wisely.

Let us keep our home and bodies free from all toxins.

Let us do that which is for our highest good.

Let us be in tune with Nature and each other

Protect our family near and far

Let us be a part of the healing of the planet.

We pray for the air and waters to be clear

We pray for peace in the world

And that MAAT will be restored to the planet once again

Ashe Amen Ra MAAT

By Kajara Nia Yaa Nebthet

Oath to the Ancestors

O Ancestors Blacker than a thousand midnights Afrikan Ancestors!

It is You who we, your children, give respect and honor

O Ancestors! We call upon you and welcome you in this place.

Afrikan Ancestors! Let your presence fill this place

O Ancestors! Who have been purposely excluded from the history books, so that the world would not know of your greatness.

Our Afrikan Ancestors! who gave civilization to the world.

Our Afrikan Ancestors! Who gave the arts to the world.

Our Afrikan Ancestors! Who gave music to the world.

Our Afrikan Ancestors! Who gave the sciences to the world.

Our Afrikan Ancestors! Who gave mathematics to the world.

Our Afrikan Ancestors! Who gave medicine to the world.

Our Afrikan Ancestors! Who gave literature to the world.

Our Afrikan Ancestors! Who gave philosophy to the world.

Our Afrikan Ancestors! Who gave God consciousness to the world.

O Ancestors we thank you for devoting your lives to make a future for us, your children, grandchildren and great- grandchildren.

Now stand with us, strengthen us, guide us, teach us and protect us from the snare of our enemies.

Rise up O Afrikan Ancestors, and let our enemies be scattered! And give us the wisdom and boldness to stand up to our oppressors and those who would hinder the liberation and empowerment of our people.

Rise up of O Afrikan Ancestors and live in us.

We will not fail to honor you!
We will not fail to respect you!
We will not fail to hear you!
And we will not betray you!
Ase

By Dr. Ray Hagins

Ancestors Libation

Praise and adoration to the Highest known by many names in which all exists

I pour and give praise and adoration to the Deities known by many names: Orisha, Neteru, Abosom and the names I did not call because I don't know your name at this time.

I pour and give praise and adoration to our celestial ancestors who belong to our Soul families: I thank you for your love and protection

I pour and give praise and adoration to our ancient ancestors who left writings on the walls, mounds, statues and literature to ensure that we don't forget the ways of our ancestors, who left the model in which we live our lives today

I pour and give praise and adoration to our close bloodline ancestors, our Maternal and Paternal ancestors.

I call on you at this time so I may honor you with this token of water (say the names of your ancestors)

I pour to my spirit guide/s I honor you, thank you for your love and protection as I give love and protection in return. Thank you for your guidance and steering us in the right directions. Without our spirit guides many of us would not be on this path at this time.

I honor all our elevated ancestors who lived their lives in a righteous way, who stood for what they believed in no matter the obstacles in their way: I honor you

(say the names of your elevated ancestors)

I love and adore my Healer ancestor who passed on the tradition of healing their children and children's children, we honour you.

I pour this token of water for the future generations so they can pour for me as I pour for my ancestors today.

I thank my animal spirit guide and the mineral kingdom

Love, honor and respect to our warrior ancestors who fought and gave their lives for the survival of their lineage, and ways we honor you.

I salute the elements air, fire water, earth, ether and Sekhem.

I salute the direction, north, south, east, west, up, and down, as well as our inner and outer.

By Ethereal-Chanie (Netret Pekh Ramu)

Libation Chant

Standing on the sacred ground that supports all life,

We honor the divine presence of the sacred spirit in all existence. We are one.

We pay homage to our spiritual guides who walk with us each day guiding and supporting our sacred journey on earth. We give thanks for your patience, wisdom, and protection.

We pay homage to the grandmothers and grandfathers

On whose backs we stand today.

We are the sum total of all those who have come before.

We pay homage to the descendants and those who have yet to come.

As you were, you shall again be

May you walk in light

We honor the continuum in the circle of life.

We give thanks Sacred Spirit

For the lessons learned and blessings bestowed in our lives.

We give thanks for the sacred ceremony we are called to celebrate today and we invite you to join us in the physical realm.

We call forth the following (At this point allow people to call forth elevated ancestors- meaning those who have lived an honorable life. After every name whisper, Ashe)

As hands and hearts are joined, Let love always be the glue that binds.

Ashe

By Ayele Kumari

Libation for African Goddess

In the name of the Great Mother Divine who comes as the Goddess within in all forms I call your names:

IYAMI AJE OSHORONGA, MOTHER CREATOR

NUT, MAAT, AUSET, SEKHERT, SHEKMET, HET HERU OF KEMET, NANA BARUKU PRIMORDIAL MOTHER OF THE YORUBA

MAMI WATA, NANE ESI, NANA SOONKWA, MAMI SIKA, ABENASIKA, ASASE YAA of the Akan

ABREWA-Primordial Mother of the Akan

OSHUN, OYA, OBA, YEMAYA of the Yoruba

ALA of the Ibo people,

MINONA, MAWU, GBADU, of the Dahomy,

DVIZA of the Shona,

POMBA GIRA of South America

MELLA of Zimbabwe,

NOWA of the Mende,

MBABA MWANA WARESA, INKOSAZANA of the Zulu

THE SHEKINAH, HOLY SPIRIT, MARY THE MOTHER, MARY THE TOWER, of the Hebrew

KALI, DEVA, DURGA, AMA, LAKSHMI, of Indus Kush

In the spirit of our Ancestral Grandmothers, we call your names

Nzinga, Queen Mother of Angola

Yaa Asantewaa, Queen warrior of the Ashanti Nation

Nefert-tari of Kemet

Nandi, Mother of Shaka

Makeda, Queen of Sheeba,

Het Shepsu-t of Kemet
Tiye of Nubia,
Come forth mothers from the Americas
Harriet Tubman,
Sojourner Truth,
Madam C J Walker,
Mary McCloud Bethune,
Zora Neale Hurston,
Rosa Parks,
Harriet Jacobs,
Phyllis Wheatly,
Ida B Wells,

We call the Big Mamas, the Madias, the Nanas, the Amas, the Iyas, of our mothers, and our mother's mothers, Dem Sisters that plowed the fields, nursed the children, the midwives, the kitchen alchemists who made the worst food taste damn good.

We call the ones who scrubbed the floors, who took the lashes, who lost the babies, who drowned themselves rather than be a slave.

We call on you today to borrow your wisdom, your knowledge, courage, your power, your beauty, your truth, and your light.

Your daughters of the new land are crying. Your daughters on the continent are dying.

Let the mothers, the grandmothers return……We need you.

Mama we need you to help us fight this fight against the destruction of our communities.

We need you to stand on our brothers that they may do right by us and our children.

We need your light because we are getting tired of holding up the race and carrying this heavy burden.

Our Sisters need you great mamas to help us stay strong and hold on to our power.

We need your healing mother for our wombs are sick, our breasts are stagnant, and our hearts are heavy.

On this day we, as a collective of women, invoke your power. We are seeds of your seeds.

Our wombs are from your wombs, we nurture from your breasts of life. We bathe in your loving grace.

We sing in your voices, we pray with your faith, we mother our children as you have mothered us. Ase

Speak to us, Guide us, forge the path for us,

Defend our backs when others come to abuse or destroy us.

Open our eyes to have eyes to see.

Open our ears to have ears to hear.

Open our hearts for true love of ourselves and others.

We give thanks Mama. We give thanks for your DNA.

We give thanks for your births, your creations, your earth where we stand.

We honor you in our dreams and waking state.

You, the mothers of all creation, the queen of queens, the warrior goddess, the portals of death and rebirth, the crossroad guardians, the love weavers, the creatrix, the Matrix, Matter (Mata-Mother).

Ase

By Ayele Kumari

Prayer of Libation

To the Essence of I AM

An ode to those that came before

I express genuine love and adorations for the foundation upon which I stand Give thanks

To the ancestors whose names I know not -

The ground swells with salt water from your tears, the trees grow from the cultivation of your spirit.

In everything I am surrounded by, I recognize you and your impact in all doings.

I pour my libation in your honor;

I sing my praises giving honor to you that my days will be long in the Land of the Most High, Selah.

In the midst of continual turmoil I am lifted to higher ground by your very presence

Calling upon your Spirit, I am surrounded by your supportive love.

Untouched and unscathed, walking in your precepts I am enlightened and humbled by your ageless wisdom.

Be the prominent and continual voice of wisdom in my right ear.

Lead my thoughts and actions to benefit your works and efforts

Let my life's work be acceptable in your eyes

Selah Ashe

By Odessa Queen Thornhill

Prayers for Special Areas

The Need for a Mother's Prayer

Many people think that prayer is just useless words with no real spiritual power. To the contrary, the power is in the word itself. When the word or sound is multiplied by intention, it activates movement in the universe. A mother has a special power to activate the word to create... Her words can create what she will. It is always important to be careful of your emotional state to ensure balance and peace so that when you speak you bring blessings to people, yourself and your family.

Ancient Mothers, especially elders and grandmothers, were vehicles to provide psychic protection for the community and nation. Mothers have a unique responsibility to offer prayers of protection and blessings to her descendants and family. As she does so, it strengthens them and empowers them with her ashe, or spiritual power.

A Mother's Prayer

SACRED SPIRIT who comes as all things to all things.

I align my heart and my mind to you.

I stand (or sit) in stillness as I call down your divine power and send it forth to my self, my descendants, and my family.

I issue forth a prayer for protection to each of them. surround them with light and love.

I issue a prayer of prosperity and abundance to them. May they use it wisely and be blessed.

I issue forth my hand to send healing energy to them.

Fill them with wisdom and knowledge SACRED SPIRIT.

(You can then say special request for specific family members.)

On this day, I give thanks as I send my ashe..

Let it be done.

By Ayele Kumari

Praises of Adoration

Giving thanks for all things great and small.

For things that create and sustain my happiness in the form of all experiences, lessons and gifts equaling positive and perceived negative.

I am grateful for people, places and opportunities being revealed and the opportunity to unlearn habits that no longer serve my highest good.

I am Grateful for experiences that support new understanding and growth.

I give thanks

Calling upon the essence of Ancestors and Spirit Guides that stand beside, behind and before me leading the way

I summon your presence and grace with wonder in my heart and glory in my mouth, I honor you.

I offer my thanks giving, I offer my body temple, I offer my respect and love

I ask that you guide my thoughts and deeds as appropriate, that my actions reflect the highest good.

I pray a yielding spirit to hear your sacred inspiration.

I pray a clear mind to acknowledge your inspiration.

I pray an unadulterated Will to fulfill your inspirations.

Moving forward in my every day habits counting the blessings and the continual support.

Thank you for your presence in my life

Ashe

By Odessa Queen Thornhill

Rising Prayer

DUA NTR

DUA RA

DUA RAAT

DUA (deity of the day)

Most High I give thanks for this new day.

I give thanks for abundance, harmony and love.

I give thanks for Mama Earth and pray for the healing of her energies.

I pray the laws of MAAT be restored within the world and in my life. I pray for divine guidance, divine protection and divine order in my life and all those that need it.

I pray for health and vitality for myself and all those that need it.

I pray for divine clarity in my decision-making.

Please empower me today, to create the righteous life I want for myself and my future generations.

DUA SHEPS

ANKH UDJAT SENEB

AMEN RA

By Damaris Amachee

Rising Prayer

I give thanks for life

I am grateful for the Light coming through my window announcing the dawn and the rising of Ra/Raat

I am grateful for this brand nu day and nu beginnings

I am grateful for breathing in and breathing out deeply and slowly

I am grateful to see the sun RA rising in this morning

I am grateful to be able to observe the creation of this nu day

I am grateful because it is where my inspiration comes from

I am grateful that my eyes are wide open to look at this colorful scene

I am grateful for feeling alive and this Divine Energy

I am grateful for being in excellent health

I am grateful for the birds who sing

I am grateful to Shu for the fresh air

I am grateful for all the Nature which awakens at the same time as me

I am grateful for Light and softness

I am grateful for feeling that everything is going be all right

I am grateful for all the discoveries and mysteries of this day

I am grateful for having such a wonderful view from my window

I am grateful for the sweet promises that reserve this journey

I am grateful for all the positive people I am going to meet today

I am grateful for staying and feeling at peace while looking at the trees and their leaves

I am grateful for all my blessings

I am grateful for everything that I forgot to be grateful for and especially the little ones

I am grateful for being me

I am grateful for who and what I am becoming

I am grateful because every day I have the chance to experience a rebirth

I give thanks for my life and all the lives around me

By Hidaya Nehanda Sanasnu Amensuat

PRAYER OF GRATITUDE

Benevolent Universe you are awesome

You answer the call of my heart without hesitation!

Beloved Goddess of Nurturing, Love and Joy,

Your blessings in my life have been abundant! I thank You!

I know That All my Ancestors, Spirit Guides and Guardians see me.

I know Your Will is being done even as I take this breath, the breath that continues to sustain me;

Keeping me whole, serving me with your protection and guidance.

I Thank You, Thank you, Thank you.

When the clouds of confusion and delusion become present in my life, You are there to bring the light of your sustaining presence

I thank you RA/RE, I thank you, thank you, thank you

When I feel limited by life, You are there to remind me that all things done in You are limitless and abundant.

On this day, I see the presence, power and love of You in all things.

I know that Your Will is at work in my life for my highest and greatest good. And for this I am so very grateful.

TUA NTR

By Sherihat Ampesh Re

Prayer Of Reflection

OH ALL OH OVERSOUL, I look at how far You've brought me, and where You're taking me, and my heart just wants to say thank You.

Thank You for showing me the beauty of my becoming.

As the veil of ignorance has finally been removed I finally see myself as worthy and enough.

I see myself as a beautiful light of Your creation in this dimension; born into this earthly realm to stand in absolute Truth.... I Am as I Am and God is.

Through my cosmic record staring into the crystal of my lives, I see a glimpse of the divine purpose You have for me, the experiences from which I must learn in this life.

I am good.

I see myself as divine perfection.

I am growing and evolving into the truth of who I Am.

I see joy and love when I look into the window of my eternal soul, my eyes.

I am learning, moment-to-moment, to see my divine higher self.

OH ALL OH OVERSOUL OH DIVINE SELF OH EVOLVED ANCESTORS

I look to You

I lean into You

I kneel before You

I offer you my offerings of gratitude and thanks

I wake up with the vibration that I am joy I am light And I am balanced living in peace.

And all is I AM

TUA NTR

By Sherihat Ampesh Re

Divine Spirit Affirmative Prayer

We recognized that there is only ONE.

As we are a part of that ONE we know for sure that there is no time, no distance, no space between us.

My breath is you and with every breath I rise higher into transcendental bliss.

We invoke healing in our hearts that we may show love where there was anger, hate, or hurt.

We call forth our divinity for we know that this is who we truly are.

Seed of your seed, we are made in your image Divine.

We pay homage to the Ancient Mothers and Fathers on whose backs we stand.

We are the sum total of your DNA and we give thanks. (Add ancestors you choose).

We give thanks to those whose names we never knew who still carried the burdens of a stolen but not forgotten people.

We pray for those who crossed during the middle passage .

We humbly acknowledge our ancestors and guides knowing that they paved our way.

It is on their backs that we stand here today proud, strong, victorious emerging ever so higher, our spirits rising to the sun.

We are the sum total of those who came before us and with that we carry the wisdom of the ages deep in our souls.

Let us invoke the GODDESS, CHRIST, AUSAR, BUDDHA, NOMMO, NYAME, OLUDUMARE within us.

Let us bring forth the sacred text we carry in our DNA.

May our children reap the blessings of our toil as we have of our mothers and fathers.

We give thanks today...

Ashe, Amen,

Let it be done and so it is.

By Ayele Kumari

PRAYER FOR HEALING

Heal my pain
Heal my wound
Water my spirit
Place me in a cocoon

Cleanse my mind
And erase all kinds
Of terrors and aches
That I can no longer take

Remove impressions that involve fear
And brought so many tears

Heal my pain
Heal my wound
Make me whole in your cocoon

Create me anew
Then set me free
To fly about
Yet grounded like the trees

Guide me, O Spirit
To your sacred space
Make my journey
A loving place

Secure me, O God
In your healing grace
Make me know
That it's not a race.

And that the victory
I have surely faced.

By YenNefer MA'AT

Prayer of the Healer

Repeat the names of your Vodouns, Neteru(s), Loas, Orishas (3 times)
Me, ...(say your Khamitic Afrikan names)
I ask for the Light because I am the Light
I wish to be in constant connection with the elements and the divinities which surround me.
....................(name all your Deities, Vodoun, Loas, orishas)
I thank all the Divinities which accompany me and for their guidance and their blessings.
Whatever happens I stay concentrated and centered.

Me, ... (say your Khamitic Afrikan names)
I Am in perfect Harmony with myself and the Universe.
I live in perfect Harmony with my real Nature and my Culture
I live and work in perfect Harmony with my divine mission.
I am a Queen and a Khamitic African Goddess.
I am a Healer.
I am a Medecine Woman.
I am a spiritual and peaceful warrior.
Me, ... (say your Khamitic Afrikan names)
I accept the Best manifests in my life.
I pray for what is the Best for me.
Love, Happiness, Wellness, Harmony, Joy, Peace, Serenity
Prosperity and Abundance are necessary for my balance.
I pray to be more than ever attentive to my intuition.
I thank the Vodouns and the caring Ancestors for their presence, their guidance and constant protection.

Me, ... (say your Khamitic Afrikan names)

I am called to help others, my Family, my Community and my People.

The more I enlighten them, the more I am enlightened.

I ask that my Spiritual Renaissance allows me to bloom and to achieve daily and completely, in full quietude, my life mission.

ASHE, ASHE, ASHE

I demand healing for myself, ... (say your Khamitic Afrikan names)

I demand Healing for ... (say the names of members of your blood family)

I demand Healing for ... (say the names of someone you care about)

I demand Healing for ... (say the names of someone who asks your help)

I demand Healing for all our children, parents, sisters and brothers who are suffering

I pray for improving the living conditions of my people worldwide

I pray for the total physical, mental and spiritual liberation of All the Africans

I pray for the African Renaissance

I pray for the resurgence of African wisdom

I pray that we continue to honor our Ancestors

I pray that we continue to perpetuate our ancestral culture and traditions.

I thank ....my teachers, my mentors, all those who guide me on this path. (you can name them)

ASHE, ASHE, ASHE !

By Hidaya Nehanda Sanasnu Amensuat

Prayer for Ancestors

I give thanks and praises to my benevolent ancestors

I thank you for protecting me

I thank you for walking with me

I thank you for showing me the truth

I thank you for teaching me discernment

I thank you for keeping me alert

I thank you for reassuring me when I thought there was no way out

I love you infinitely ancestors for all that you endured so that my life on this plane is filled with lessons that could never be taught from a book

I praise you benevolent ancestors

I honor you benevolent ancestors

I appreciate all you do in my life and I continue to gratify you in the most sincere way

Ashe

AMEN RA

MAAT

By Sherihat Ampesh Re

PRAYER FOR HEALTHY DELIVERY

MOST HIGH MOTHER FATHER DIVINE CREATOR

Duau

Give thanks for this ancestor making its way into this realm

Bless the limbs of its physical body

Bless this being as it comes forth with a message

Purified in the body of water it journeys in, sending healing vibrations into the Universe

Safe delivery through the canal of the womb within which this life force was held

As he or she makes their entrance preparing to take their first breath

may this be done with ease as intended

Knowing that all is in perfect Divine Order as the way opens and the vessel expands releasing this being

In sync with the ebb and flow of this body making gentle shifts to emerge

May each push be grounding and freeing

Mother Father Creator bless this space for entry

purifying all those present.

We receive with humility and Divine love.

AMEN-RA

By Empress Tabia "Khet Ra MA'AT"

Prayer for Living with Purpose

MOST HIGH MOTHER FATHER CREATOR

I surrender

Rid me of my ego

Allow me to receive in a state of pure and unconditional love, the Divine that works through me

Emitting frequencies and vibrations, attracting what is needed to carry out the plan according to you Divine Mother Father

Grant me patience in the process as it emerges into sight and physicality from the ethers

Humbled I am, to be chosen for this mission and I remain steadfast taking my steps with complete

conviction and surrenderance

I receive

I receive

Eye receive

Delivering that which has been bestowed upon me, to others

In grace, light and ease

DUA NTR

By Empress Tabia "Khet Ra MA'AT"

Prayer for Safe Travels

DIVINE MOTHER FATHER CREATOR

As I embark upon this journey

I walk with purpose

A path is cleared for safety to and from this Divine mission

Along the way may I connect to the beauty in all things

May the path be sweet and the days be blissful

May I receive all I cross paths with in love and light

As the journey becomes a sacred memory I give praise and thanks

Knowing each step I've taken was in perfect MAAT

DUA NTR

By Empress Tabia "Khet Ra MA'AT"

PRAYER FOR THE ROAD (OR FLIGHT)

Thank you my Ancestors

For protecting me on this road,
Go and return

Of all the dangers,

Visible as invisible

Of the speed, the violence and the alcohol

Thank you for accompanying me

throughout the day

Thank you for protecting our children

and all those who will also use this road today

Ashe, ashe, ashe !

By Hidaya Nehanda Sanasnu Amensuat

PRAYER FOR CLEARING OBSTACLES

Ankh Udja Seneb

Divine Creator allow me to unstick that which has become stuck

Allow me to release that which needs to be let go

Allow paths to emerge that I may have glossed over

May I shift my perception and my burden become light

May I welcome much needed changes in my relationships

May I accept things as they are and not as I think they should be

I humbly let go of drive of the ego

I humbly let go of intentions of the selfish

I gratefully accept my life just the way it is and isn't

I gratefully wait in patience for that which I can't understand

I love all those near and from a distance who came bearing lessons

I give thankhs for all the lessons I've received and accept the Master plan

I am at peace with things that didn't go as my two eyes saw

My heart is light and I am free

I am whole, all pieces restored

Divine Mother Divine Father,

may all be cleared which I've harbored

I am at peace

I am clear

Dua NTR

By Empress Tabia "Khet Ra MA'AT"

Prayer Before Eating

Thank you CREATOR/CREATRESS, and my Ancestors

For blessing this meal

The hands who have prepared it,

The hands which have planted and harvested

these fruits and vegetables to feed us.

That we give and share with those who do not have

That this meal give us all the strength and energy needed to accomplish our missions

That this meal regenerates our cells

We give thanks and praise because everyday we have enough to sustain us on this table

Thank you Mother Nature

Thank you Mother Earth

For offering us these fruits and vegetables

Thank you and let us remain ourselves and in excellent health

Ashe, Ashe, Ashe

By Hidaya Nehanda Sanasnu Amensuat

Prayer Before Eating

We thank you GREAT SPIRIT
For bringing this meal to our table
Bless the many hands that have touched this food
Bless this meal
And may it be nourishing
For our Bodies,
Our minds and
Our Spirits.
Ashe

By Kajara Nia Yaa Nebthet

Prayer for Spiritual Bath

Chant, pray and sing while making the bath

I call forth the GREAT SPIRIT and the Great Mothers of the Waters
I ask you to bless this bath with your love and healing light
May this healing bath be purifying to my mind, body and spirit.
May this water heal and clear my aura
May this water clear my heart
That I may feel lighter
May this water clear my eyes so I can see more clearly
May this water clear my ears so I may hear when my Spirit Guides speak to me
Dua, thank you

While bathing pray and chant

I release all blockages and negative energy
I release all fear
I release all worry
I release all stress
I release all that blocks me from moving forward
I release all that blocks me from my higher self
I am clear
I am healthy
I am whole
Thank you Great Spirit
Thank you Great Mothers

By Kajara Nia Yaa Nebthet

PRAYER FOR DIVINATION

I call forth THE MOST HIGH
KNOWN BY MANY NAMES
AMEN, OLUDUMARE, NYAME
Creator of All things
Let your Divine light shine through me
I call my Great Spirit guides to speak with me
Help me Great Spirit Ones
Help me to see
Show me what I need to see
Give me the answers
Show me the way
Let me know what is going on with (say name)
On this Day

Use this before doing tarot or other forms of divination.

By Kajara Nia Yaa Nebthet

PRAYER FOR SMUDGING

May my mind be free from the worries of the world.

May my voice be heard to speak out against injustice.

May my arms be open to give love,

and may my heart be open to receive love.

May my will be strong

and my creativity flow.

May I be rooted and grounded to the earth to receive all that she has to offer.

May my back be protected by those who love me

and may I let go of all those things that do not serve me.

Asé

AMEN-RA, MAAT

Say this prayer as you smudge yourself/others with sage following the pattern of an Ankh around your body

By Aqseshsha Asu-At

Prayer for Smudging

We give thanks for your beautiful and Divine Spirit.

We pray that you may release all the cares of the world.

Release all worries, doubts and fears.

Release all anger and other negative emotions.

Be light, be free

Be open to receive the messages and blessings that are for you to receive on this day.

May your steps be divinely guided

May you always be on your right and divine path.

May this work be for your highest good.

Dua NTR

Ashe

Start at the top of the head and move down around the body in the form of an Ankh, ask one to hold their arms out to the side while smudging. Do the front of body then the back and under each foot.

By Kajara Nia Yaa Nebthet

Prayer before Resting

We thank you GREAT SPIRIT and Great Ancestors
For walking with us on this day
We thank you for your many blessings
We thank you for protecting us day and night
Let us rest well
Let us be ready for a beautiful day tomorrow.
DUA NTR
ASHE
AMEN RA MAAT

By Kajara Nia Yaa Nebthet

Prayer before Resting

MOST HIGH

I ask for your guidance and protection as I dream and my spirit travels.

May all the energies that I encounter be of and from the light with positive intentions and high vibrations.

I ask my benevolent righteous Sheps, Spirit Guardians and Spirit Guides to block all negative entities from being present in or near my auric field.

I pray my spirit returns safely to my body.

DUA NTR

DUA NUT

AMEN RA

By Damaris Amachree

PRAYER FOR ABUNDANCE

We come to you humble this evening and in prayer for the upliftment of our communities

and for our families, children

and for our own spiritual preservation.

We ask for guidance to help direct our minds, and spirit in reconnecting with our truest selves,

to know and to believe that our bodies are sacred vessels,

that our wombs are the...

homes of the souls returning.

That we are not without fault,

but we must begin to forgive ourselves and others for any transgressions known and unknown.

We pray for healing of our bodies, our spirits, and our minds.

We pray for the upliftment of the children, that they will be protected, nurtured and loved.

Please fill us up with joy, good health, hope, happiness, peace of mind, good character, gentle character, self love, self determination, moral courage, self-worth and unity

Please fill up our purses with prosperity, wealth, and abundance. Then say: (fill them up, fill them up, fill them up) (then say your confirmation statement)

Best to say this at the full moon, the first night. Go outside hold up your purse, wallet, suitcase up to the moon and say "fill em up" three times.

By~ OOL-Osaremi and OAA -Iya Olusoga

PRAYER FOR ABUNDANCE

MOTHER FATHER CREATOR
Great Forces of Wealth and Joy
May you bring wealth to my home
May you bring wealth to my door
May you bring wealth to my pockets
May you bring wealth to my family and friends
May you bring wealth to my business
May my work bring great rewards
May my mind overflow with creativity
May the work of my hands bring money for my family
May I have all I need to expand and grow financially
May I have all that I need and more to take care of myself and my youth
May our home always be full of joy and harmony
We thank you
We thank you
We thank you
Ashe

By Kajara Nia Yaa Nebthet

Prayer for Positivity

I pray that I think peace, speak peace

and I AM peace

I pray that I think truth, speak truth

and that I AM truth

I pray that I think love, speak love

and that I AM love

I pray everything I attract

carries high, harmonious vibrations and intentions.

May the light within me serve

as a beacon for those that need it.

AMEN-RA

By Damaris Amachree

Prayer for a Divine Mate

DUA benevolent, righteous SHEPS

I pray to the spirit of

(any grandfather ancestor that was married and known to be righteous and benevolent),

That you guide me towards the man/woman that is my divine mate.

I give thanks for my divine mate and the divine, crystal children we will bring into this world.

May our union help to heal all wounds from past relationships.

DUA (ancestor's name)

DUA HET-HERU

DUA SHEPS

AMEN RA

Make offerings to the ancestors throughout and after the process and continue to give thanks

By Damaris Amachree

Prayer For family Unity

MOST HIGH MOTHER FATHER DIVINE CREATOR

May balance be restored to the family structure

May the parent be restored as the child's primary educator

May new generations of crystal children be raised on whole, highly vibrational, pure foods

May the village system be restored in our communities

May our young people, all accounted for, journey through inherited rites of passage emerging with the stories of the Ancients

May our roots be grounded and sustainable, every harvest bountiful

May Divine love be the foundation of every home

May melanated beings reunite seeing themselves whole in one another

May all imbalances be made balanced, inside and out

May all children be raised with a complete sense of self from whole parenting

May forgiveness be practiced daily

May 'hoods be made clean and free from all cides

May we come together in peace and harmony with a complete overstanding of who we are and what we're capable of

May the legacy of our Ancestors carry us along

Most High we TRUST

Dua NTR

By Empress Tabia "Khet Ra MAAT"

PRAYER FOR GLOBAL HEALING

Sacred Mother Earth,

As planetary healing takes place, may the shifts be gentle for all

Allow natural beauty to be restored once again in and for all

As natural resources flourish bountifully, may starvation and lack be healed with abundance

May an end be put to an advantageous government

May we grow in harmony and respect our fellow human

May human beings unify beyond self-imposed classifying demarcations

As lost cities reemerge, may we as sentient beings master the oneness of coexistence

May language be used as a tool, and no longer abused

May we forgive the stories of long ago because we are no longer robbed of the present

Sacred Mother Earth,

As your core ways open, may those transitioning travel safely to other realms

Sacred Mother Earth,

As you make shifts, may your bodies of water be healed capturing the frequency of love

By Empress Tabia "Khet Ra MAAT"

May the crescent be restored to fertile ground free from poisonous toxins

May the air in which we breathe be sweet, and free from harmful gas

May we as beings of this time respect the space that has been granted to us because it is sacred

May we forgive unto ourselves for what has passed knowing all was in MA'ATIAN order

AMEN-RA

AMEN-RA

AMEN-RA

By Empress Tabia "Khet Ra MAAT"

I AM

I am a Khamitic African Goddess

I am a brand nu Divinity

I am a warrior and glorious soul

And I believe in it

It is from my soul and spirit that will come the almighty

Because I become what I am thinking

I am Precious

I am Divine

I am Love

I am Free

I am Luminous

I am Natural and Spiritual

I am full of Energy

I am radiant

I am combatant and militant

I am brilliant and gifted

I am courageous and determined
I am omnipotent and omniscient

I express it because all this is in me

All the knowledge, power and strength are in me

Thanks to the knowledge, teachings and lessons that I acquired near my Ancestors, Elders, my mentors and my descendants.

I express it because all Africa, KMT, Mother Earth is in me

I am a nu Khamitic African Goddess

I act with Truth, Humility, Sincerity and Modesty

I am an Absolutely Unique Being

I am incomparable

Because now I am myself

I am………………………………………………… (say your Khamitic African names)

Ashe, ashe, ashe !

By Hidaya Nehanda Sanasnu Amensuat

We Are

We are Khamitic African Goddesses

We are brand nu Divinities

We are warrior and glorious souls

And we believe in it

It is from our soul and spirit that will come the Almighty

Because we become what we are thinking

We are Precious

We are Divine

We are Love

We are Free

We are Luminous

We are Natural and Spiritual

We are full of Energy

We are radiant

We are combatant and militant

We are brilliant and gifted

We are courageous and determined
We are omnipotent and omniscient

We express it because all this is in us

All the knowledge, power and strength are in us

Thanks to the knowledge, teachings and lessons that we acquired near our Ancestors, Elders, our mentors and our descendants

We express it because all Africa, KMT, Mother Earth is in us

We are nu Khamitic African Goddess
We act with Truth, Humility, Sincerity and Modesty
We are Absolutely Unique Beings

We are incomparable

Because now We are ourself

We are and I am.. (say your Khamitic African names)

Ashe, ashe, ashe

By Hidaya Nehanda Sanasnu Amensuat

Prayer for my People

O GREAT SPIRIT

Who gives life to All

We come to ask that you bless our families

Bring good health and sweetness into our lives

Bless the Mothers and surround them with love

Bless the Fathers and let them be fully present for their families

Bless the Sisters and let them support and love each other

Bless the Brothers and let them use their energy wisely

Bless the Children and let them be divinely guided and cared for

Let us remember our purpose for being here

Let us remember the ways of our Ancestors

Let us make wise choices and decisions

Let us be protected at all times

Let us overcome all obstacles

Let us be in tune with our higher selves

May we all be a part of our healing by correcting ourselves

And may MAAT rule and live within us once again

Ase

May it be so

By Kajara Nia Yaa Nebthet

Meditation

Meditaion

We pray to the Divine. The Divine communicates with us through meditation. Generally, the purpose of meditation is to cleanse the subconscious mind of negative thoughts and attachments—to purify the mind. With the addition of hekau or mantra repetition (words of power) added to a meditation, liberation or the acquisition of higher vision while still alive is possible. We open the way for a connection to Infinity in which Infinity can talk to us.

For most of us, stilling the mind for meditation is not so easily accomplished. We often have a multitude of thoughts running through our head upon rising in the morning until we close our eyes for sleep. Even then our mind may flit from one subject to another before we finally drift off. Just as our physical body needs rest in order for it to function optimally, so, too, our mind needs a break from the constant inner chatter. In addition to opening a way for the Divine to communicate with us, meditation also gives our mind relief from the babble.

Meditation is a process. A meditative mind must be developed. First, we have to still our physical bodies. Sit up comfortably and straight. Lying down may invite sleep. When the body is still, the mind can become still. Next, we have to let any thought that comes pass by. We may acknowledge that the thought is there but we must gently let it go. With practice we will come to a place of peaceful silence of the mind. This is meditation. A still body + a still mind = meditation. Meditation is a gradual process. Try stilling the mind for a minute, then two minutes, then three, eleven minutes—until meditation can take place for an hour or even more. This place of stillness will be one that draws us to it. We will want to be in that place regularly. It feels good. It is restful. It is peaceful. It is refreshing.

Once the meditative mind is developed, the intuitive mind can be developed. We are already intuitive to one degree or another. With a meditative mind we are able to *really* develop our intuition to the extent that we can tap into it and get the answer we need to any given question. Yes. We can develop our minds to that capacity. What we must do is be still and listen to our inner voice. It will be the voice of our own positive self. This capacity comes to us when we master our mind through meditation, when we can still it at will, have no incoming thoughts. Our mind is with us then. Most of us let our mind master us. We must master our mind, let it serve us. When we master our mind we can direct it. We can develop and work that time that our mind is with us. We can focus our energy, manifest. We can connect to our soul.

Mantra allows us to develop a meditative mind immediately. Mantra is a positive sound and thought. The thought should be of high vibration. It should be a thought that is held in very high regard. It should really resonate personally. It should fill the heart with its power because it means so much. This will make it possible to tune in and move the vibration from the thought to the subconscious level. Mantras are chanted to create positive results quickly. There are some powerful mantras out there. They can assist us in releasing blocks, fears, and unconscious demoting habits that inhibit our spiritual growth.

To experience the spiritual flow of the meditative mind is what we seek.

By Mut Shat Shemsut

Light Meditation

Sit comfortably in an upright position, feet flat on the floor, back straight.

As we enter into this meditation I want you to close your eyes and visualize. See yourself in your inner eye as your whole body being the light that lights the darkness.

As you see yourself illuminating you inhale. As you inhale visualize the spark of life entering into you. It's lighting up your very being.

You are illumination, inhale and exhale slowly.

Exhale all of those things which feel like and look like death in your body, inhale and exhale.

Now

As an illuminated, being in the darkness you look beyond yourself and see a tree, a tree that is filled with the light of life. You are sitting in front of this tree. Your light is connecting to the light of the tree.

Visualize, connect and feel the spiritual light veins of the tree connecting to your spiritual light veins.

As you connect with this tree you're inhaling and exhaling more deeply and letting go of all negative thoughts, feelings, pains and ego.

Release as you exhale and inhale more positive light-filled energy. As you inhale you are expanding.

Exhale, inhale- you are expanding

You are growing, you are realizing that You are an infinite being, You are an infinite light that is shining.

Exhale all limitations, inhale. As you are expanding you are becoming more balanced, more grounded and more secure in the self.

Exhale, feel secure, feel grounded. Feel full of light, empowered to move with right action.

Inhale deeply. You are seeing yourself filled with light and connected to the Source.

Say to yourself

I am a divine being of light
All that I wish to manifest is mine
I am divine love
I am divine manifestations of my oversoul powers
Love and divine light lives and flows through me
I am that am

You may want to record this to make the process flow, and to allow you to focus on the meditation.

By Sherihat Ampesh Re

Kundalini Yoga Meditation

This meditation will revive your mind by addressing negative thought patterns, or, those that are troubling, persistent, or obsessive. Note that in some Indian traditions Ganesh is regarded as an elephant-headed god who is called upon to remove obstacles.

Tune in with the Adi Mantra: ONG NAMO GURU DEV NAMO (DEV rhymes with save) Chant 3 X

Breath: Long and Deep
Sit with a straight spine and with the eyes closed.
Think of a troubling thought.

Mudra: The left thumb and the little pinky finger extend out from the hand. The other fingers are curled into a fist with fingertips on the Moon Mound (the root of the thumb that extends down to the wrist).

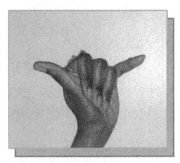

The left hand and elbow are parallel to the floor, with the tips of the left thumb pressing on the curved notch of the nose between the eyes.

With the right hand and elbow parallel to the floor, grip the little finger with the right hand and close the right hand into a fist around it. Both hands now extend straight out from your head. Push the notch with the tip of the left thumb so that you feel some soreness. The soreness will decrease after continued practice. Breathe long and deep.

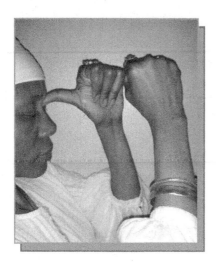
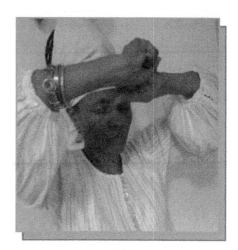

Arms are parallel to floor

Time: Do this meditation for 3 minutes. <u>No longer</u>.

To end: Maintain the posture with eyes closed. Inhale. Push a little more and pull the Navel Point in by tightening the abdominal muscles for 10 seconds. Exhale. Repeat one more time.

Close with the words SAT NAM (Saaaaaaaaaaaaat NAM) 1 to 3 times

Ganesha Meditation for Focus and Clarity

Yogi Bhajan, May 1997

Submitted by Mut Shat Shemsut

MEDITATION FOR PROTECTION:

SAY THIS KUNDALINI YOGA MANTRA

Around the House - (3 Times) Every Day.
Around the Car - (3 Times) before, you drive, anywhere.
And Teach it to Your Children
So They can say it
(3 Times) around themselves, before going out

(on a date, for example)
or riding with a friend.

AAD GURAY NAMEH

JUGAAD GURAY NAMEH

SAT GURAY NAMEH

SIRI GURU DAYVAY NAMEH

(SIRI is pronounced CITY)

Translation

I BOW TO (OR CALL ON) THE PRIMAL WISDOM.

I BOW TO (OR CALL ON) THE WISDOM THROUGH THE AGES.

I BOW TO (OR CALL ON) THE TRUE WISDOM.

I BOW TO (OR CALL ON) THE GREAT TRANSPARENT WISDOM WITHIN.

Submitted by Mut Shat Shemsut

Final Thoughts

AFRIKAN PLEDGE

We are Afrikan People

We will remember the humanity, glory and suffering of our ancestors, and honor the struggle of our elders

We will strive to bring new values and new life to our people

We will have peace and harmony among us.

We will be loving, sharing, and creative.

We will work, study and listen, so we may learn,

Learn so we may teach

We will cultivate self-reliance

We will work to resurrect and unify our homeland

We will raise many children for our nation

We will have discipline, patience, devotion and courage

We will live as models, to provide new direction for our people

We will be free and self-determining

We are Afrikan people

We will win

This is one of the pledges said to help encourage Nationbuilding and dedication within our community.

Author unknown

Pray.

Many people just don't.

And when they do, it's within the confines of a church setting, or their minds. When you examine the etymology of words, church translates to a place to learn. Hence the liberation experienced when people come together to learn what it means to tap into spirit, collectively and individually.

As Afrakan people, we have been so far removed from naturally convening with spirit and see access only through the systems of church. What if you saw access through yourself first?

The Divine is within you. This is why meditation is so popular. It is your time to speak with spirit and to allow spirit to speak with you. When you close your eyes, it's you, your essence, your 'I am', it's the Most High within you.

For some of us, closing our eyes includes the stream of our thoughts and worries. This is normal considering how inundated we are with data on a day-to-day basis. It's in this space that one can bear witness to just how distracted they are/can be. What a perfect clearing/space for Sacred words!

Divine, Most High Creator, may we worry not because we are here to be a happy, vibrant, fruitful people.

When you start to utilize prayer, and integrate the philosophy of the power behind word, then you start to (re) connect to the Divine essence that exists in you and us all. It knows no race, creed, or color.

By Empress Tabia "Khet Ra MA'AT"

It's funny, when Nia told us that Ra Sekhi would be writing a book of prayers I thought, Yes!

Then No...

I want to contribute but where do I start???

I can start with praying for an end to oppression.

I can start with sick elders and sicker youth.

I can send light to the sisters and brothers looking post-war for a victory that is not theirs.

A Mer and an Ankh to the centers of the communities where officials present themselves as law and order violate the order of law.

A Hotep to the keepers of our stories, the shoulders we stand upon as ways are opened for us to live what has been prophesized

Live what has been prophesized

An Ankh, Udja, Seneb -may we experience as we come together and balance frequencies of distrust, jealousy, generational ways of being that we're accustomed to learning, with the higher frequency of MAAT

An Ashe because it is done.

Ashe because it is done.

Ashe because the time has come.

By Empress Tabia Khet Ra MA'AT

We give T'Ankhs, Honor and Praises to those who made contributions to this book.

Aqseshsha Asu-At
Ayele Kumari
Chief Ifadunke Olayemi, Yoruba Kabbalah
Damaris Amachee
Deborah Gear Iya Adel'oni
Empress Tabia Khet Ra MA'AT
Ethereal-Chanie (Netret Pekh Ramu)
Hidaya Nehanda Sanasnu Amensuat
Khinuu Nefer
Kwesi Ra Nehem Ptah Akhan
Mut Shat Shemsut
Odessa Queen Thornhill
Qamarah Muhammed El Shamesh
Ras Ben
Rekhit Kajara Nia Yaa Nebthet
Sherihat Mesut Besarta Ampesh Re
Tchiya Amet
YenNefer MA'AT

Special Thanks to our Esteemed Elders who gave permission to include their work

Dr. Frances Cress Welsing, M.D.,1996
Author - "The Isis Papers: The Keys to the Colors"
With permission given April 21, 2014

Dr Ray Hagins, founder of African Village
With permission given April 21, 2014

Babalawo Modupe Opeola from Ile-Ife, Nigeria, West Africa.
Ebuibon Awoyinfa Abereifa

For information about
Ra Sekhi Arts Temple
Our books, products and classes

Visit us Online
www.rasekhihealing.com

For our blog and products visit
www.rasekhistore.com

You can also Follow us
Ra Sekhi Arts Temple
On Facebook, Twiiter, Instagram and Youtube

Also by Ra Sekhi Arts Temple

Ra Sekhi Kemetic Reiki Level 1

Ra Sekhi Kemetic Reiki Level 2

Recipes for Elevation

I Get Energy from the Sun

Made in the USA
Las Vegas, NV
07 November 2023